THROUGH THE COVID LOOKING GLASS AND BACK

Traci Ciepiela

ISBN 979-8-89112-957-3 (Paperback)
ISBN 979-8-89112-958-0 (Digital)

Copyright © 2024 Traci Ciepiela
All rights reserved
First Edition

All rights reserved. No part of this publication may be reproduced, distributed, or transmitted in any form or by any means, including photocopying, recording, or other electronic or mechanical methods without the prior written permission of the publisher. For permission requests, solicit the publisher via the address below.

Covenant Books
11661 Hwy 707
Murrells Inlet, SC 29576
www.covenantbooks.com

1

TODAY IS THE DAY I DIED

Today is the day; it is a year after the day I died. Or I guess "nearly died" would be the correct description. I was in respiratory arrest and nearly unconscious. I don't have any idea how I even woke up that morning. I never should have been able to open my eyes. I knew the night before I had a pretty good upper respiratory infection going on, so that night, I decided I was going to use my oxygen concentrator just to give me a little bit more oxygen while I slept. I assume that is the only reason I work up on this morning a year ago. If I had just turned over, to go back to sleep that morning, I would not be here anymore. A lot of people over the past couple of years have been in this position. I survived; many didn't. But I sometimes question whether it was a good thing. I do wonder if I am really one of the lucky ones.

When COVID first hit the world, I didn't really think too much of it. I actually was over on that side of the world enjoying a trip to New Zealand for the new year. I had no idea that a deadly virus was spreading unabated in that corner of the globe. I flew home from the trip and went back to my job, and my life never even hearing the words COVID or coronavirus. That would change.

Shortly after returning to the US, I actually did get very sick. After being sick for a couple of weeks, I went to the doctor and asked for antibiotics because whatever I had wasn't going away. Even with a full course of antibiotics, the illness did not abate, and I remained sick for another couple of weeks. So when news of COVID broke, I believed I already had an early version since antibiotics did nothing to kick the illness I had. I would eventually find out that you can get COVID again.

As businesses shut down in March of 2020, it felt like COVID was going to infiltrate my community like a huge cloud of death chasing people down the street, and if we dared to be outside it would engulf us, killing everyone in an instant like a bad horror movie. My work actually ended up moving online. I was able to continue teaching for the college I work for, and I was able to continue receiving an income. If I had been one of the unlucky ones to lose my income, I don't know what I would have done. How does one live without an income when there are bills to be paid?

In reality, that cloud I expected to chase me down the street never did emerge, but after a few months of dealing with the disease circulating around the globe, things started to open back up at least where I lived; other states weren't as lucky. It was finally June when my gym opened back up. My workplace would go to mostly in-person starting that fall.

I didn't know a lot about COVID. It really seemed no one anywhere in the world knew much about it. No one I knew had it, and from news reports of people who did have it indicated that it was similar to a cold or a really bad flulike illness. I really reached a point in the drama and the doomsday discussions on public forums where I just didn't care anymore. If I was going to get it, I was going to get it. If I didn't, I didn't. And when I started hearing people say things like you could have the virus but no symptoms at all, I really just didn't care anymore—at all.

I went back to work as did many people after five months of being "locked out of my job" being forced to work only online, only daring to visit with friends as we all got takeout together and sat in our cars separated in the parking lots of restaurants. I was one of the lucky ones because my state opened up much faster than others did, so we got to get back to "normal" by the time summer rolled around.

When we got back to work, we had to wear masks since someone thought that a cloth covering over your mouth could stop a deadly virus. We had to try to stay at least six feet apart from each other and from students. I had to remove chairs from classrooms to make sure students could also be six feet apart. I teach at a college, and we were forced to go online in 2020, and when we were allowed back, the students were given a choice as to whether or not they attended. Needless to say, college students tended to prefer staying in bed and attending class by computer. The college spent thousands installing cameras in what we would start to refer to as "Zoom" rooms. The college was very persnickety in regard to those cloth barriers too. Faculty were even getting in trouble if we didn't force students to comply as well.

Many of my students took to wearing a neck gator over our mouths and nose. At some point, and I don't know why, the college decided that wasn't enough and forced us to the masks that wrapped around your ears. They also spent a lot of money purchasing N95 masks and sending them to us through interoffice mail. I never even opened that package I was sent as it was stamped with "Made in China." I had no desire to put that on my face. Not to mention all the videos posted on different social media outlets showing grotesque conditions in which masks were being constructed.

Living alone, like I do, the lockdown, the lockout, really got particularly hard for me. My gym was closed, work was online, and the only time I saw anyone was when I did the parking lot lunch circle or when people walked by my house walking their dog. I started to take joy in just watching the little kids across the street enjoying themselves while they played in their front yard. It was like the world had ended and no one told me. The joy of watching kids play though was short-lived. Being alone and being sequestered resulted in an immense feeling of isolation and depression.

I definitely did get accustomed to the ability to sleep—a lot. I also became an expert in binge-watching shows on Hulu. I lucked out that there was something like twenty-seven seasons of the *Amazing Race*. Fourteen-hour long episodes, at least, in each season, for twenty-seven seasons. I spent most of the lockdown in bed or moving ten feet to the couch to binge-watch TV. There was nothing open; there was nothing anyone could do. All we could do is stay still. I read a lot as well when I got tired of TV, but the solitude of the "two weeks to slow the curve" turning into five months of isolation, got the best of me; and I simply just didn't care anymore if the virus got me and killed me because what I was doing wasn't a life worth living. What I was doing was simply just existing.

I never lived my life like that. I don't just exist. I like to stay busy, and I like to have things to do. Watching TV, while it happens to pass the time, isn't having something to do. I eventually took some time to knit scarves, the only thing I can seem to be capable of knitting and even worked on some embroidery. I made an assortment of baby gifts, engagement gifts, and I even finally opened up that last pillowcase set I bought more than a decade before and started to embroider all those tiny flowers.

When the weather got a little warmer, I was at least able to go out and ride my bike on one of the numerous trails in the area. I was so glad I wasn't in one of the states that actually felt a need to close trails and beaches that resulted in arrests of people who were engaged in some kayaking by themselves or fishing. It all seemed so crazy.

That cloud of virus didn't chase me down the street, but the virus did eventually come to my doorstep in September; I got sick. At the time, word of the supposed deadly "Delta" variant had been circulating in the news. I assume that is the one that finally managed to find me. Of course tests really never tested for variations whether it was Omicron or Delta or Beta or anything else; the tests just showed SARS-COVID 19.

I will never actually know where or how the virus invaded my body, but I do know somewhere around the beginning of September, the virus crawled its way into my body and the result wasn't going to be easy. It was, in fact, going to start an entire malevolent chapter in my life, which I am still living in. I've had difficult times before; this time was going to be potentially more than what I could survive on my own.

I developed symptoms somewhere around September 10, 2021. My biggest assumption at the time was that I didn't have COVID. I was actually under the impression that I had a very early strain of it years ago; and I didn't know, at that time, you could get it a second time. There was never much in terms of clear information as to how the virus presents itself. It seemed like this virus could appear as anything.

I didn't think I had any of the beginning signs or symptoms of the disease. From what I had heard, it sometimes starts with a sore throat or a headache, but I didn't have a sore throat. I didn't have a headache; I didn't lose taste or smell either. I had a little bit of a fever and developed what I believed to simply be an upper respiratory infection. I generally get sick with a respiratory infection every year, so it didn't surprise me that I was feeling that familiar burning in my lungs. I usually have a low-grade fever with it as well so that didn't concern me. I figured I would just be ill for a week or so, and it would get better. I was wrong.

I called in sick to work on Monday and Tuesday of that week, when I woke up Wednesday, I knew something was different. I got up and tried to get to the bathroom, just that short walk left me sucking air, trying to breathe. I made a phone call to a friend who told me that maybe it was time that I call 911 when I explained to him how much of a problem I was having breathing that morning.

I decided I would call an ambulance or drive myself to the hospital, but first I had to do a few things. I needed to make sure the windows in my house were closed because it was supposed to get hot, and I needed to be sure the air was on for my furry animals. The process of closing the eight windows in my house took way too long and took way too much energy. I barely remember, but I am pretty sure I had to stop to try to get a good breath of air into my lungs a couple of times. That should have been a warning sign to call faster. But I just continued my list of things I wanted to do before I left.

If I was going to go to the hospital, I might want a bag in case I have to stay, and I might want some things with me. In hindsight, I didn't pack nearly enough, and I would have to ask friends to deliver things to the hospital to try to make my stay there a little more tolerable. I packed some things and then, just like you always want to wear clean underwear in the event you are in an accident, I decided that I needed to brush my teeth before going out. After all, I had woken up about two hours before this point, and I couldn't let morning breath affect those who would be treating me in the hospital.

When I got into the bathroom to brush my teeth, that was the first time I saw myself that morning. That's when I realized just how much trouble I was in. I looked dead. My skin was gray, and my lips were blue; it was like looking at my own corpse in the mirror. I didn't realize until that point that I was suffocating to death.

After rinsing my mouth of toothpaste, I grabbed my bag then I grabbed my phone. I dialed 911.

I told the dispatcher I couldn't breathe and gave them my address. I even told her that I had planned to drive myself to the emergency room but that I feared I would pass out before I got there. The ambulance is only a couple blocks away, so it only took a minute for them to arrive outside.

I grabbed my keys, my bag, and I stopped and took one last look around at my house because I didn't know if I would ever be back. The thought was almost too much for me. I was about to walk out of the door of the place I called home with all my worldly possessions for the last three years, and I closed the door, locking it behind me, leaving my furry family members inside. It broke my heart to walk out of the door, not knowing if I would ever see them again. It is a difficult realization, all the things you treasured, all the creatures you loved were being locked inside a house that I might never return to.

I worried about my cats. Living alone, they are my constant companions. Usually, when I am going on a trip, they know I am leaving because they see me packing, they try to get in the way of me packing by getting into my suitcase and making a bed for themselves. This time, though, I walked out of the front door without ever packing a suitcase, and I didn't return for a week.

I know they had to be confused and scared. It breaks my heart to this day that I might never have seen them again. That they would be cared for in my house by friends until my mother or sister could arrive and eventually take them back home with them after handling my estate. They wouldn't understand where I went or why, and they would have to go somewhere that was unfamiliar to them with unfamiliar people and probably a lot less attention than they were used to.

My sister would have taken very good care of them, and strangely enough, I had already prepared for them in a will I put together years before, but they would be packed up and moved halfway across the country to live with people they never met and didn't know. My pets are my support system and my constant companions, and I was about to leave them possibly forever. The idea just broke me.

At least I was going to get a chance to live by making that 911 call. Of course, going to the hospital at that point was a fifty-fifty type of situation; of those who wound up on ventilators, many times, they never recovered. Whether I survived remained to be seen. The alternative would have been that I died that morning, and eventually one of my friends would have had to discover my body. I don't know what kind of effect that would have had on my family, my cats, or my friends.

As I tried to walk out of my front door to meet the paramedic, he asked me if I could make it to the rig parked right in front of my house. I handed him my bag and my phone since I was still on the line with emergency dispatchers.

I don't have a large yard, but that morning, the ambulance may as well have been at a marathon distance from my front door. Even with the help of the paramedic, I couldn't walk to the ambulance door. I almost fell on the front lawn. I stopped to try to breathe. Somehow, I managed to walk the additional steps I needed to get in the ambulance door. I think the paramedic, after seeing my gray skin and blue lips, was pretty desperate to get me into the rig; he probably pulled me the rest of the way.

I don't remember a lot from that point on. I heard the paramedic say that my oxygen level was at sixty-five. I remember telling them which insurance group I was with. I recall the paramedics discussing which hospital to take me to and them deciding on going where I asked since my medical records would already be available to the doctors. I finally had oxygen given to me. Nothing in my life had felt so good. I seemed to be getting some oxygen into my system for the first time that morning without the struggle. I closed my eyes; I heard the siren, and suddenly, I was at the hospital. The trip was only seven miles. I don't remember a second of it.

Upon being rolled into the hospital emergency room, I heard the paramedic mention that they had managed to get my oxygen level up to 80 percent on the way into the ER. I actually felt a little comforted with that number. Being someone who deals with upper respiratory infections every year, the eighties is a commonplace for my oxygen level to be especially when I am sick.

Suddenly, there were nurses sticking IVs, grabbing clothing, putting my bag somewhere in the room, and then the tests started. Of course, the COVID test that we are all so familiar with today was one of the first things they did. I was eventually sent for a CAT scan. I was entertained by the nurses who discussed how they were going to get me onto the scanner bed. I told them that I could walk, and I would be fine. I would just get up and sit down on the scanner bed for them. I think I generally surprised them that I was capable of doing just that.

After returning to the emergency room, a doctor showed up, whom I hadn't seen yet; he asked me when I had been diagnosed with COVID. I don't know if I even answered because up until that point, I still was thinking it was just an upper respiratory infection. So I told him, "I guess now," and the doctor walked away. I remember seeing him one more time a couple hours later he told me that I was in very critical condition. If I didn't improve quickly, I would have to be put on a ventilator, and I was very sick.

The last sentence didn't even need to be said; the sheer fact that I was in the emergency room, I knew I was very sick. I am not the type of person to run to the doctor every time I have an ache or a pain. I definitely don't willingly go to the emergency room without a dire situation. I even usually wait a full week after getting an upper respiratory infection before calling the doctor because it is more likely that I can get medication for it since it's been lingering that long. So I knew I was very ill.

I wasn't living in a media blackout or anything. I knew having to go on a ventilator was pretty much a death sentence; at that time, very few people ever made it off a ventilator. I thought about my life in the time I had before being moved to a room. I thought about all the things I had done. I knew at that point I really didn't have a bucket list that I needed to do. I had been around the world a couple of times. I have lived all over the country. I had three specific and different careers. I was over fifty.

I knew if the situation developed, I would say no to a ventilator, and if oxygen couldn't save me then perhaps my life has run its course. I would dearly miss my pets, but I decided that I would say no to a ventilator. I had no desire to be put into a coma and having tubes shoved down my throat to breathe for me. If this was going to be my end, I wanted to go conscious and aware.

The interesting thing is that the thought of dying that day didn't scare me. I wasn't sitting in that hospital bed pleading with God to give me more time. I was at peace. I was understanding that this could be it. I didn't mind. I have said for years prior to this, I have done more in my lifetime than some people manage with two. I had no regrets. With the exception of a couple guys, I should have kissed and a few I wish I hadn't, there were no regrets in my heart. I had no sadness about it at all. I had no fears as to what was coming next. But then, I also realized that I chose to call 911, I willingly came to the hospital for treatment, and I willingly let the hospital treat me.

I realized; I chose to fight, and I chose to live.

2

THE HOSPITAL

I was eventually moved into a room on the fourth floor of what is called Allen Hospital. I had a window that looked out over a parking lot. At least I had a window. I was hooked up to all kinds of machines that beeped and sounded alarms when my oxygen level fell below 80 percent, which was all the time. I struggled to breathe most of the first couple of days. I laid in a bed, visited by nurses, and every couple of hours, I was given all kinds of medications to take, although I had no idea what they were. I was given bags of IV fluids, also with no idea what I was being given.

To this day, I am not really sure what all the medications I was given were. I was just given little cups full of pills every twelve hours or so. Along with my regular medications, I have no idea what I was taking. I do know I was put on the Remdisivir protocol. I only know that because I saw the IV bag on the fifth and final day of the regimen. I am not normally the type of person to just take medications without knowing exactly what I am putting in my body. The treatments weren't discussed with me. I didn't have any idea what was being pumped into my system. I had no idea the effects they might have on me.

Throughout the past year I learned all kinds of things about Remdisivir and none of it was good. There is even a class action suit happening against the company that made the drug. Apparently, some of the batches had glass shards in it, others suffered severe kidney or liver damage resulting in deaths and injuries. I don't know why I was spared those things, at least to this point. I have no idea if this drug has any long-term side effects.

There are a lot of reasons I am very careful as to what kind of drug is put into my body. You see, I am a redheaded genetic freak of nature. In order to be born to parents who both have brown hair, I was blessed, or maybe *cursed* is a better word, with all the recessive biological traits of both parents' genetic strains. I don't react very well to the side effects to a lot of medications. So typically, before I will agree to take any kind of medication, I need to know what the side effects are, and I usually will decide as to whether or not I am willing to risk those side effects. In the past, I had side effects not even listed on some medications.

If I knew then what I know now about the Remdisivir, I would have said no. I was too sick, though I didn't get the chance to agree or disagree. I was really at the mercy of the doctors, who, as history has shown were at the mercy of the CDC, ultimately Dr. Fauci and his directives.

When I finally got to the hospital room and was allowed a moment to myself, I found my cell phone, and I texted my friends: "I'm in the hospital. I have COVID. If I don't survive, cremate my body. I don't want a funeral. Can someone please take care of the cats?" Looking back, I probably should have tried to stem the blow of that information. It shocked everyone. Sadly, they all had to go get their own COVID test due to the close contact I had with them just five days earlier when we went out for lunch.

I later found out my friend Staci was in a drive-through at the time the text arrived, and she couldn't order because she had no idea that I was even sick. I didn't really feel like sending any other texts because I was tired.

Staci and another friend Cindy took turns caring for my cats; my friend Jane called my mom every day to try to keep her in the loop, not that there was a lot of detail to share. I was in and out of consciousness really for the first couple of days in the hospital. I recall very little. The only thing I had to keep me occupied was the TV. I got to rewatch a lot of *Supernatural, Charmed, Friends,* and other assorted shows. There was nothing else I could do but sit in that bed try to breathe and keep my oxygen level above eighty to avoid the alarms sounding and sleep.

Most of the nursing staff at the hospital were truly wonderful. None of them judged me, with the exception of one nurse. He came in for the night rounds just as I was about to fall asleep one night. His name was Jim, and he was mean to me. I am sick, and I definitely don't feel well. I don't need someone to act like a jerk. He seemed to want to argue with me over how I slept. I have always been a side sleeper. I don't sleep on my back, which is what he seemed to think I was doing. He seemed to insist that I somehow sleep on my stomach, which he insisted was better for me. He made me feel so horrible, as if I didn't feel that way already.

I had things taped to my chest; there was a whole telemetry box strapped to my chest. Exactly how did he think I would be able to sleep on that? I'll admit I am not always the best patient, but I try to be as pleasant as I can, but he was pushing my buttons. I wanted to tell him to lay off it was my life and death if I so choose for it to be. Besides, my stomach also ached from the shots I had to take to prevent blood clots; Heparin hurts.

Every day, I had to take hot burning shots into my stomach to avoid blood clots. I am not afraid of needles, and I don't mind the whole "getting stuck" part. It was the searing burning pain that came once the substance was injected. It didn't last long but long enough to know that I did not like getting those shots. The bruises that developed around my abdomen where the shots went in were also not a pleasant feeling.

Most of the staff were great, and there was even one nurse who came to hang out in my room with me while she did all her notes for the day so we could chat. I found her really sweet and fun, and she enjoyed the conversation as well. All my other nurses really did a great job in a very trying time for me. COVID patients weren't allowed visitors, and the emotional toll that takes on a person while sick makes it even harder to recover. The only contact I really had the outside world was through a phone; how intensely lonely that is. As if the original quarantine when COVID first arrived, now I am in a second and left pretty much alone.

I did eventually see the first nurse I had later in the week. I asked because I am a curious person if he thought he would see me again. He told me honestly that he didn't think I was even going to survive that first night in the hospital, let alone a few days and then actually apparently starting to get better.

As I spoke with all the nurses and technicians, many of them did not get a vaccine either. Many of them had COVID themselves.

On my third day in the hospital, my doctor felt I was out of immediate danger, but that I was going to be in the hospital for a little while longer. I wasn't yet off heavy doses of oxygen. I had yet to get out of bed to move further than two steps to the portable toilet without my oxygen level dropping below eighty. I had quite a way to go before I would be well enough to go home.

My friends were able to get to my house and pack some additional things for my stay like one of my pillows and a blanket to make my stay a little more comfortable. Because I wasn't allowed visitors, they had to drop my items off at the emergency room to be sent up to me sometime later that day. I was never so happy to see my pillow or my blanket. Hospital pillows aren't my favorite nor at the blankets, so I was very happy to see the package arrive in my room.

It was during that third or fourth day when all was quiet in my room that I started to think about life again. I realized in the way this world works today, so many of my acquaintances and friends would never know what happened to me without someone getting onto my Facebook page to let them all know. I felt really horrible that some of my friends would have to find out about my death over Facebook. I know just how awful and jarring that could be.

I've learned of a couple of my acquaintances passing away over Facebook, and it is never an easy feeling. One was just a casual friend, someone you would say hello to occasionally, but the other was a former student of mine who was very near and dear to my heart. I couldn't have imagined not knowing but having to find out in such an impersonal way hurt more than having someone let me know personally.

Some of the people who are very important to me don't live locally where I do so other than Facebook, there would just be no other way they would know. I don't have any belief that my life is so important to all those people, but I know I am important to at least some on my Facebook friends list, and they would want to know. There would be no way for my family or friends to be able to find the phone numbers of all those people, and so Facebook would have been the only option. It made me sad to think that people wouldn't know anything other than COVID took me.

I didn't want to be classified as one of those people who had "comorbidities," which I do, but I didn't want to be classified as one of those people who died from other causes and just happened to have COVID at the time. I really would have wanted people to know it was the virus that was claiming my life if it did. Even with the comorbidities I have, I always worked very hard to not let those things shorten my lifespan.

The fourth day in the hospital during the morning visit from my nurse tech, I informed him that when he was done with his rounds, I was going to go for a walk. Whatever he had to do, he needed to get things ready and rigged up so I could get out of bed and walk down the hall. I was going to go for a walk. I needed to move, I needed to get back on my feet.

Sometime around noon, he came back in, and we got the mobile oxygen tank ready; he found my slippers, which I hadn't seen since I walked out of my house days earlier, and I put my feet on the floor to walk. What I thought was going to be a wonderful excursion outside the room I have been shut up in for days turned into something else entirely. I was astounded at my lack of ability to even walk down the hospital wing hallway. I had only been bed ridden for a few days. The walk lasted maybe five minutes total. It was so short.

I had been biking up to forty miles a week and swimming nearly five miles a week just prior to being sick. I was capable of walking a few miles. I had even started to try to reintroduce jogging into my work out routine in the weeks leading up to getting sick and now, I couldn't even make it down the hallway of the hospital. COVID seemed to eat away every bit of muscle I had. This was not a side effect I had heard about from anyone, anywhere.

I anticipated being able to walk around for thirty minutes or so, this first go-around. It wasn't the oxygen that was the problem either. I just seemed to have no muscular control suddenly. Every muscle in my body had been wiped away in that one week with COVID. How could that be? I almost fell a couple of times during that short walk. More importantly, I was emotionally devastated, I had been working so hard and for so long, and it all seemed to be gone. I had little balance. I had little in the way of stamina. I was a triathlete before I got sick, and now everything seemed to be gone.

I had surgery, and I was in the hospital overnight more than twenty years ago. Hours after surgery, I had the desire to get up and walk around. About three in the morning, I was just itching to get up. Honestly, I walked that hospital floor for over an hour, I was still in pain and had to move carefully to avoid tweaking the massive number of stitches I had. But it felt wonderful to get up and out of bed. This same feeling is what I expected to be able to do this time as well. Yes, I was about twenty years older. Maybe I would only walk for thirty minutes. I couldn't do it. I barely made it down the hall. It was hard on me emotionally.

I didn't understand. How could I go from being able to do so much to being able to do so little? It was devastating. Athletic capability does not come easily to me, and I've had to work very hard to get to where I was, and it seems with one virus everything had been wiped away. It was difficult to take. I once managed to complete an Olympic Distance Triathlon, which was all about grit and determination, and now I was diminished to not being able to walk twenty feet.

Not only was it emotionally draining to know I could barely walk anywhere, the thought of having to try to build up again to my level of fitness felt like a wave of despair rolling on in as if there was a hurricane in my soul.

I discovered a second time just how incapable I was of any kind of ability to walk when I was released from the hospital later in the week. When I got home, there was just one small step up to my front door, and I stepped up, but my leg didn't have the ability to straighten out. I almost fell off the front porch, which no doubt would have sent me back to the ER since I would have fallen headfirst into a bed of rocks. I asked the friend who brought me home to stay in the house just for a little bit so I could take a shower in case I fell. How could this be happening?

No one knew much about this virus and all of the things it does, and I don't think we still know all the things it has done to people. I know to me it somehow destroyed all the muscles in my body. I wonder to this day how much if any brain damage was done by the virus and my low oxygen levels. Today even years later, I still sometimes forget words and names. How much damage was done? I don't know. I don't know if I will ever know the scope of it all.

I also don't like to tell everyone the problems I am experiencing. I want to be able to continue to live a life and that means I need to keep my job and I need to keep living where I am. It has been more than just forgetting words too. It has expanded a bit. I was confused recently as to where I was. I was simply filling out a form, and I couldn't get out of my head that I was in a different city and a different state and lived at my former residence. I don't understand why that happened. It only happened once, but it scares me to think I might not be able to live on my own at some point in the future. At that point, I'm not sure where I would go.

On day 5 in the hospital, I was "stepped down" to a nasal cannula as opposed to the bi-pap I had been using. Instead of heavy doses of very humid oxygen, I was stepped down to about five liters of oxygen, which is about double room air. I still needed the additional support for my lungs for the time being. Later that night with the pneumonia letting go of my lungs, I was moved down to four and then three liters.

I was able now to make it to the restroom in the room. I no longer needed the porta-potty. I also took the opportunity to brush my teeth. There had always been a sink with a mirror in front of it in my room. I could always see the mirror from my hospital bed, but I never looked in the mirror. The image I held of my corpselike face the last time I looked in the mirror made me afraid to do it again. I didn't want to look in the mirror and see an image that unnerved me like it did a few days before.

I finally took a look as I brushed my teeth. Gone were the blue lips and the corpselike color, but what remained was someone I didn't even know. COVID may have stolen my lungs for a week, destroyed all the muscle I had, and now here was the evidence that it had walked all over my face as well. Gone was the person I thought I knew, remaining in her place was someone that seemed to have aged decades in five days. I didn't see me anymore; I saw someone who seemed to be so much older. I didn't look like myself anymore.

It was difficult to see. It was still much scarier to see my death mask from earlier that week, but I looked so old, so haggard, and just decades older.

I did have a good conversation with the doctor on duty day 5 though. I pushed him and requested he consider sending me home sooner than later. I was getting antsy sitting in the hospital bed. It was uncomfortable to sleep there. I was afraid of the physical problems I was having and how I would deal with it at home, but I didn't want to be in the hospital anymore.

The doctor agreed that patients can only get "so well" in the hospital setting, and at some point, I would need to go home and prove I could keep my oxygen levels up with just my home oxygen concentrator. On day 6, the doctor agreed to send me home. I was so happy, and yet there was a strange feeling that I was experiencing, although I didn't yet have a name for it yet.

That feeling would become clear in the near future.

3

Going Home

I managed to beat a virus that should have claimed my life. I was a survivor; I was a victor or at least I tried to tell myself that. While in the hospital, there was another patient in the hospital with COVID on my hall. He was double vaccinated and boosted, yet he passed away while I somehow managed to survive. I learned one of my friends was willing to pick me up to take me home. This was going to be my first chance to actually see someone I knew since before I got sick as well. I exited the hospital for the first time in almost a week, and my friend Staci was right there to collect all the belongings and to get me home.

I wore a mask out of the hospital and the entire ride to my house just to be safe. When I got home, I almost burst into tears. The home that contained my cats was in front of me, and I was actually coming home when I didn't think I would. I walked away from this house almost a week prior, honestly believing I'd never see it again. All I wanted to do was to get inside and understand that I truly survived, and I was back with the two furry creatures that mean everything to me.

I got into the house and discovered that my friends had not only taken care of them, but they also did so much for me. They did my laundry, did my dishes, and cleaned up for me. When I left, I had been ill for a few days so there were dishes in my sink and things were just a little unkempt. There was even still laundry in the dryer when

I arrived. I was so thankful for everything they had done. I could be in my house and relax instead of trying to do laundry myself. The bedsheets and pillowcases would be something that I would have to change out, but they already did that for me. I could just be home. I asked my friend to stay until I could take a shower in case I fell in the bathtub. There was no telling how long my legs would support me yet.

I was so happy to see my cats. Of course, they were perfectly fine; my friends had taken very good care of them, as I knew they would. They stuck very close to my side after my return. They missed me, and I missed them. Coming home to them helped me to realize that I was living in reality and not comatose on a ventilator somewhere and dreaming. They helped bring me back to life.

It had been a week since I was last able to shower. I was offered the opportunity to do so in the hospital, but I couldn't since the shampoo and the conditioner that the hospital was offering were going to be items I would be allergic to. Again, my red headedness was going to come into play. I am allergic to very strange things and smells are one of those things. So the first thing I wanted to do when I got home was to get in the shower.

I know based on my career and field of study that individuals lose about one hundred hairs a day. As a former police officer, it is one of those things you learn especially when you have evidence to collect at crime scenes. My hair was generally tied up into a ponytail or a bun the entire hospital stay. The amount of hair I pulled out of my head in that first shower was just shocking to me. I had never seen the handfuls of hair that I now held in my hands.

Little did I know that the handfuls of hair I lost that day were not going to be the last of the hair I lost. One of the side effects no one ever talks about with COVID is losing your hair. Typically, two to three months after a case of COVID, your hair falls out. No one prepared me for this. In November, when I started pulling handfuls of hair out of my head, I freaked. I didn't understand. I finally had a chance to ask the doctor who finally informed me that the hair loss was a side effect to COVID and could happen with any major pneumonia.

When I talked to others, many of them informed me they had lost their hair as well. Hairdressers were seeing a lot of hair loss in clients.

My hair was one of the most important personal physical attributes I possessed; if I do say so myself, it was beautiful. It was down to the small of my back. I had been growing it for four years. It was curly red hair that was really my shining glory. I was not gifted in the looks department, but I was gifted with amazing hair and now I was losing it.

I can't pull off the bald look. I cut it short in an attempt to see if the lighter weight would maybe allow a few strands to stay in, with no luck. It kept falling out; I developed some bald spots. I was devastated. I started wearing a hat in November and had to wear that hat on and off for a year. To date although my hair is growing back in, I still have shorter hair growing in with the longer hair, and it is just a mess sometimes. Not the crown of glory I've had my whole life.

My hair is growing in curlier than it already was, which I don't mind; but the shorter, curlier hair often tangles with the longer straighter hair. I can barely even really pull off a ponytail because of all the shorter hair falling out or sticking out. I am still hoping that one day it will return to its previous glory. Although I have been told that hair rarely returns as thick or as colorful. So I wait, and I will see.

That first night sleeping in my own bed was not as wonderful as I thought it would be; sure it was so much more comfortable than that hospital bed, but what I realized is that my brain had gotten used to the interruptions of my sleep at midnight and at 3:00 a.m. when nurses would stop in to check on me. I actually remember saying to myself when I woke up in the middle of the night that I might as well stay awake since the nurse will probably be in momentarily and then I had to remind myself I was home, and there wasn't a nurse coming to wake me up.

The next night, I woke up and didn't know where I was. I had gotten so used to the hospital room; it was strange being in my own bed. I didn't recognize my room, and I looked for the same hospital window I looked out for a week, which was no longer there. Eventually, after a few days at home, sleeping got more normalized.

When I talk to others about the long-term COVID side effects, they often talk of brain fog and a myriad of different side effects. My longer-lasting "aftereffects" seem to be on the rare or different side. I didn't feel like I had brain fog. I know I had a tendency to forget words or struggle to come up with words at times. Maybe that is what they were referring to as brain fog? I'm not sure. It was surely a sign that the low oxygen levels at the start of my hospitalization may have caused some brain damage.

What I was experiencing though was a "needles and pins feeling" in my lower legs. It wasn't painful, but it was a strange buzzing feeling in my lower legs. I didn't have a lot of control over my legs, and I couldn't really feel my legs from the knee down, just that strange buzzing feeling. The feeling lasted for weeks. I don't even really recall the day that stopped, but I know I was still experiencing it almost two weeks later on my birthday. I didn't feel overly "well," but I didn't really expect to.

It was an odd day, my birthday. I had made it past fifty. Just a few weeks before hand I didn't think I would make it past the fifty years I had been alive. The trip I was on when COVID started to spread was a trip a friend of mine and I had planned long ago. We both had birthdays in October, and we both had planned to take a trip for our fiftieth. We ended up doing the trip when we were forty-nine heading into 2020 instead of the end of 2020, which, in hindsight, was a good choice since we wouldn't have been allowed to travel at the end of 2020. If we hadn't gone early, I might have also missed the opportunity to see and experience New Zealand. So when I turned fifty-one, I just had this feeling that it was unreal.

I was almost gone at fifty. I had been a police officer for fourteen years and managed to avoid any major injury. I had moved states away from where I resided multiple times. I managed to survive fifty years, a virus really gave me a run for my money, so turning fifty-one was surreal. Whether I would survive any longer than one day into fifty-one was about to be tested.

The night of my birthday, after dinner with my friends, I was driving home when I got hit from behind. A driver most likely driving 35 mph, slammed into the back of my car as I waited to turn left to head back to my house. The driver of the car fled the scene, and because my glasses flew off in the crash, I couldn't see the license plate. I am a retired police officer, and I knew if I didn't get that plate, no one would ever find that car again. I couldn't see. I don't know if I blacked out during the crash. I was confused as to what had happened; all I remember if a very loud sound and then the seat back in my car broke. My car was totaled.

Normally, the damage to my car could have been repaired but my car was a 1999 Chevy Cavalier, which still had a tape deck, and the car was just four thousand miles from flipping to 200k. I knew the car was totaled. I also knew that I still hadn't seen a bill from the hospital yet for a week's stay with who knows what drugs and who knows what other costs. Now I was faced with having to go buy a new car the next day.

This is the event that pushed my whole body into overload, and I lost it. When the police got there, they summoned an ambulance for me because I was unable to communicate really. I know in my head what was happening, but I couldn't relay that information. I was too upset.

It was just a thing, it was just a car, but it had been my car since the day I bought it in January of 2000. At the time, it was the last car on the lot from the year before. That car had been with me through multiple moves; it had been in most of the states throughout the center of the country. I've slept in that car when on trips. I had moved from Missouri to Wyoming and then to Iowa in that car. My whole life seemed to take place while I owned that car, and now it was totaled. It was going to have to be towed from the scene. I felt as if my life was being taken away even though it was just a car. Having faced death with COVID, the car crash just seemed to tell me I wasn't yet out of the woods.

I called one of my friends from the crash site, who had just gotten home from the dinner we had. She drove right back over with her husband. The firefighters arrived at the crash scene. They were so nice to me; they even tried to pull some of the damage out so I might be able to drive the car until I could get something new.

I was so upset, though they eventually had to ask me if there was something else going on that they were unaware of, and finally, that is when the damn burst. I told them I had just gotten out of the hospital from COVID, and that I still didn't feel well. One of the paramedics who arrived at the crash scene was actually the paramedic who managed to drag me into the ambulance the day I called 911. It was very interesting running into him again at this next big event of my life.

I told them I had thousands of dollars of bills coming from the hospital, and I had no idea what that was going to be, and now I had to go out and buy a new car because my car of over twenty years was going to have to be towed to a junk yard to be scrapped for parts, and it was my birthday. The firefighter/paramedics at least wished me a happy birthday. A number of them had birthdays of their own coming up.

Eventually, my friend Staci and her husband arrived; he was recognized by the officer and some of the paramedics. Things started to calm down I was able to start thinking again.

I needed to find a way to get to work in the morning. I needed to find a rental car for a couple of days, so I could get a new car. I needed to get the title of my car to the junk yard so they could scrap it. I had to clean out my car the next day of my possessions. There was so much to do, and I wasn't sure I felt well enough to get any of it done. The tow truck arrived, and I watched my car get hoisted up onto the flatbed for its final ride to its final resting place. It was the best car I ever had. I almost had my physical life taken from me, and now another part of that life was being taken away from me.

I am not one to tempt fate and ask God or the universe what else do I have to go through? As soon as you ask the question, God shows up to prove to you how much more you can go through. I was getting very close to wondering that very thing. I had just beaten death with COVID, I still didn't feel well, and someone has to smash into the back of my car while I was sitting still waiting to make a turn?

This crash could have been much more violent and could have resulted in me being back in the hospital or even dead. How ironic that would have been? Survive COVID just to be killed a few weeks later in a car crash? I could just imagine the newspaper headline.

I wanted to scream at the top of my lungs, "How much more do I have to go through? What did I do to deserve this?" I had so many questions. I didn't shout out those words that night. I didn't want God to show up and give me more to handle. The sad part is that this chapter in my life was far from over; there was more to go through.

The accident seemed to be a catalyst. The questions were just a prelude to the things I would be thinking about over the next couple of months. The prevailing thought that started to course through my mind was, what now? I was at a complete loss for what my future should hold.

What dreams, what desires, or what other bucket list of things did I need to do? Was there some universal calling that someone was trying to get across to me? Was God trying to get my attention? I totally expected to have some kind of idea as to what I still wanted to accomplish in life or some kind of an idea as to what I am supposed to do with the rest of my life, but nothing came to mind. I have been down this road before, and so I expected to feel a push to get moving and get going on life, but nothing was coming to me.

4

History

In 2012, my world seemed to be turned upside down. I got a phone call that my dad was in the hospital, and when they finally performed an MRI, we knew he was dying. He had cancer, which they believed started in his gall bladder. He was enrolled in hospice; he was brought home, and thirty days later, he passed away in the middle of the night. I did manage to fly home to see him before he left.

Thirty days later, I had to make the decision to send my cat over the Rainbow Bridge. This cat had been with me for over seventeen years. She was such a sweet little unassuming cat. I came home one day and found her just sitting in the litter box, unable to use it. The next day, I saw her fall just walking across the floor I knew at that point it was time. Out of all the pets I've had, this was the first time I had to take one to the vet myself to give her the final kindness I could show her and put her out of her pain. I knew it would be hard, but I had just lost my dad, I hadn't yet started to handle the grief from that and now I had to say goodbye to my friend.

It wasn't long after her death that I started a relationship. Looking back now, I wonder if he intentionally saw a way to take advantage of my grief and pain. I thought that this relationship could have been the man I had been praying for. I even naively thought that maybe there was some help from my dad on the other side now, bringing this person into my life. We knew each other for quite some time. The relationship felt so right and so natural. I was in no state of mind to think about the possibility that I was only being taken advantage of.

It wasn't long before he broke my heart and stomped on it. He definitely wasn't the person he pretended to be. I don't know if he specifically was taking advantage of me, but his actions made it pretty clear that may have been his intention all along. I, of course, found out about his betrayal from someone else. When I gave him an opportunity to speak to me to say anything to me, he simply shrugged his shoulders and turned his back on me.

At the same time, I discovered his deceit. I was diagnosed with melanoma. It is a particular virulent form of skin cancer. The scary thing was I knew it had been on my arm for over five years at the point I asked my doctor to remove it. Five years, with cancer sitting on my arm. No telling where that cancer could have already spread. I might be just days from dying. Here I was, the girl who gets a diagnosis of cancer, and her boyfriend whom she thought was going to be her husband one day cheats on her. I used to love all those stories of the couples who marry even though one is dying or very sick. All those stories used to warm my heart; my story was not anywhere close to that.

My doctor removed the tumor on my arm, which led to the diagnosis, but I had to have a second removal of skin around the tumor. I was told by my oncologist that if the tumor spread, I would have to have more tests to determine the extent of the spread and I would potentially have to look at getting chemo or radiation or a combination of both. That was news that just really "topped" this year of loss, grief, pain, and sorrow—all which happened in about a six-month timeline. Before I got the pathology report back, I knew what I needed to do.

If I was going to head down the path of chemo or radiation, I wanted to make sure I got some things done first, especially if my time on the planet was coming to an end sooner than I expected. I thought about doing some crazy things people would never expect of me. I scheduled a trip to Australia, a place I've always wanted to go. I also then convinced a friend to sign up for a triathlon with me.

THROUGH THE COVID LOOKING GLASS AND BACK

I had done a triathlon race once before, but I did it as part of a team, so I only did the swim portion of the race. I wanted to do a whole race. I didn't even have a bike yet. And I coerced my friend Denise into doing the race with me, so I would have someone to keep me honest and determined. I couldn't let her down by not showing up for the race.

My triathlon career would span a number of years, I even became a race director and created a race in my home state. One of my proudest moments was finishing an Olympic distance race, even though I cut my toe open in the warm-up to the swim. By the time I finished the race, it was more than four and a half hours, and I had blood soaking through my sneaker, but I finished. Looking back on 2012, I realized, after all was said and done that year, I came out stronger with more of a purpose with a desire to live my life.

I started to travel as well. People save their entire lives to be able to travel after they retire. So often, people don't make it that long. Too often, people aren't able to enjoy traveling by the time they reach they age they can retire and do so. I was in a great position because between semesters, I was able to have a couple of weeks of time. I also had months off during the summer. I started to fill those weeks with trips around the world. First was Australia, then Iceland and Greenland. I continued with destinations like Alaska, Ireland, the Netherlands, and the Mediterranean.

Having survived cancer, in a very lucky way, I didn't want to miss out on the things I always wanted to do. So I made sure I saved and planned each trip to get the most out of my newfound opportunity.

That is why this time, this COVID experience was so strange. Here again, I was heading down a path that might mean my ultimate end, but I came through it and the only thing I felt was a big empty black pit of a hole in my head, heart, and soul where my hopes, dreams, and desires used to reside.

Now, it seemed like there was just nothing. Nothing in my head as to any other bucket list item. I felt defeated inside and out. I definitely did not come out of this life-altering event like I did in 2012; it's more than a year later, and I can't say that I feel stronger. I can't say I feel like I have a major purpose to pursue. I just still feel like a shell of my former self.

Some people might chalk this up to brain fog. Some may chalk it up to long COVID. I just think it was more likely that I wasn't prepared to survive. I said earlier that during the COVID scare, I reached a point where I just didn't care anymore. Either it was going to get me and kill me, or it wasn't. Maybe I reached a point where I was just tired of the scare and what will happen is just what will happen. Being fearful and stressed doesn't prevent what the future holds; it just holds you back from being able to live.

I am not really surprised that I didn't have a lot of bucket list items come to mind because I had been around the world twice really. I had seen Australia, New Zealand, parts of Northern Europe, Iceland, and Greenland. I've seen whales, moose, elk, reindeer, wolves, dolphins, and little blue penguins in the wild. I knew that if I didn't get a chance to travel again during this lifetime that I had seen most of what I truly desired to see.

While struggling with the aftereffects of COVID, the car wreck and my emotional or mental nothingness someone told me that I never needed a dramatic event to scale Mt. Everest. And he was right, but I had been in this place before, I just kind of expected to have some kind of inkling as to what I was supposed to do now. What mountain am I ready to climb even if COVID might be the catalyst for that adventure?

None of us need a life-changing event to finally do the things we want to do. So many people save money and put things off for "someday." For a lot of people, someday might never come. I started traveling and doing all the things that I thought about doing someday after my dad died and my cancer diagnosis; I was one of the lucky ones.

I had a big enough scare to push me into realizing that my someday might never arrive. It is true that no one needs an earth-shattering experience to plan the trip of a lifetime or to scale Mt. Everest. I was lucky to get extra time to experience things in life I wanted to. Now I have another second chance or a third chance if you will, and how many people get that?

As weeks went by, I struggled with those thoughts of nothingness. Is there a reason to go on? Is there something great waiting for me in the future? Is there some reason I was spared when so many others weren't?

An idea came to me one afternoon. I knew when I was in the hospital that first couple of nights hovering near death, I thought of all the people who were students of mine, mentors of mine who made me who I am today, heroes I worked with, and just cherished friends who were always more like family to me. I realized that none of them would know what happened to me unless someone, sadly enough, got onto Facebook to make an announcement. It is so difficult in today's world to keep up with your friends. We text, we use Messenger, but we rarely actually speak on the phone to people anymore. Honestly, I probably don't have phone numbers for most people today.

The thought of that repulsed me. I sadly know what it is like to find out when someone has died over Facebook, and while convenient, it is just a horrible way to discover your loved one is now gone from the planet. I am glad none of my close-knit group of friends found out that I died by way of Facebook, but one thing I could definitely do is tell each and every one of them how much they mean to me, how much they did for me, and how grateful I am that they were part of the tale that created my story.

I decided to write everyone I knew to be an important part of my life, a letter. Now, of course, I sent those letters via email and through Messenger because I don't have addresses of people anymore. This is the world we are now living in, unless you are very meticulous and send out Christmas cards, a lot of us have become dependent on our cell phones to remember phone numbers. We are totally worthless in remembering addresses because letters tend to be a thing of the past and today email and Messenger gives us that instantaneous transmittal.

I started at the beginning with some of the mentors and heroes from my early years. I called them my letters to my heroes. Although I am sure none of them would refer to themselves that way. I would add a lot of personal thoughts and experiences I remember. From the best boss I really ever had to my dance teacher who became so much a part of my life. I would spend days at the dance studio after school and into the evening. When I graduated and left for college, I cried because I wouldn't be part of that studio again sadly.

From the people I worked with when I was an intern at a TV station who taught me so much and made me believe I could stand right in there on my own two feet because I knew what I was doing. To some of the students I've had in class that are now doing amazing things in their own lives whether they are in the coast guard or working as a lawyer, whether they are in the military now or working in policing so many of those students are part of the best memories I have.

So many came as students, so many left as more than friends, and honestly, I haven't been prouder of anyone than I am of my former students. I cherish the thought that I was part of their story becoming who they are going to be as well. Everything comes back around. People helped me become who I am, and I have had the honor and the privilege to help do that for others.

My letters went something like this:

> I am writing to you as part of a project I have undertaken. When I got Covid back in September, I didn't think I was going to survive. Most of my nurses didn't think I would either. I was alright with the idea that this might have been the end because I have done more in my life than some people do with two, so I was good with the idea that it could have been the end. The one thing I was sad about was that I wouldn't get to say goodbye to all the people out there, who made my life what it was, is, and will be. I was sad that I didn't have the time to reach out and tell each of those individuals who helped me become the person I am, who helped with the times I experienced that were trying, and those who made my life a joy to be experiencing. I also felt bad that I was just going to disappear, and it

could be months or even years before some people ever heard what had happened to me.

But I survived. I couldn't believe it myself but somehow, I managed to go from a sixty-five on the oxygenation of my body, to eighty with about twenty liters of oxygen being pushed up my nose for days in the hospital. I eventually made it to eighty-five and then to ninety. It was only the fourth day I was in the hospital that I managed to come down to just room air being pushed. I went from twenty liters down to two, and although I needed oxygen when I got out of the hospital, still, it was only a couple of weeks, and I was back to normal. Whatever *normal* might be.

After getting home, I was left with a huge hole in my heart. I didn't know why I had survived. I didn't understand it. After other trying experiences of cancer and of being emotionally broken, I seemed to come back stronger and better and more determined to do things that I hadn't been able to do before. Or things I was putting off. I have now traveled the world, I've been around the world twice, I completed both a sprint and an Olympic triathlon, I put my heart on the line and had it broken, I had the chance to do so much, but this time I was at a loss. I really had no new goals, different dreams, new things to do. So I am writing letters.

I am writing these letters because I knew that in the hospital, I wasn't going to get the chance to. But now I have the chance so I am writing letters to my personal heroes who deserve to know how amazing they are, how much they helped me, and how much I would have missed them."

I then generally include some personal things:

Hi there, Mary Alice

    This is a private letter to you. I met you for the first time when I was just 7 years old. The Purple People Eater dance was the first. I still remember the day when I displayed some of my quirky character, my mom suggested that I really play up the "wanting to get a job in a rock and roll bank" section of that song. So I did. I always remember how much you smiled and laughed at that.

    I always remember the way you would smile when I walked in the door for dance class throughout the years. I'm sure many others had the same kind of response from you but it always made me feel kind of special and that means a lot as a 7 year old.

    Moving forward in time with the tambourine and how entertain ed you seemed to be with the number and the sizes of the bats I would bring for class in practice for the keystone cops performance. Every week I had a different color and a different sized plastic bat.

    I know you might not remember all of these things, but I do. It's amazing what you remember from 7, 8 or even 9 years old. I wanted to make sure I told you and some other very special people the very special things I remember.

    If I hadn't survived, I know there would be so many people I didn't get to say goodbye to. You being one of them of course. The year you allowed me to be a helper made me feel so amazing. I really tried and I hope you were proud of me, I did the best I could. You became such a friend, mentor and just an all around supportive person I owe a lot of who I am and who I have become to you.

Thank you for being a very big part of my life. Thank you for being so sweet to me. I always remembered my time in the dance studio fondly. So if you ever feel like you don't make a difference, you have, and you did and you continue to do so. Thank you for everything you ever taught me, thank you for being my friend.

Hi Linda,

I hope this is still a good email for you. I have started a project of sorts. I got Covid back in September, and it was horrible. When I was in the hospital, I definitely realized that this could very well be my end. I was alright with that. I knew I had lived more in my one life than some people live with two. So I was okay with the potential that I was not long for the planet. I really wasn't bothered by that. But the one thing that made me sad was all the people I would never get to say goodbye to. All the people I never would get a chance to really tell them how much they impacted my life and how they helped me become the person I am.

When I first started work at Channel 7 you were such a bright spot. Always with a smile, always so friendly. I really loved working there. I so wish I could have stayed there longer. There are a few things I always think about while working for you. The day I spilled coffee on Steve Tasker's hand. The day I met Les Nessman, the day Danny and Keith Partridge came town. I really always fondly recall the day you and Brian got flu shots live on air and then the next day you popped the bottle of "Keopectate" on the table. (not sure on the spelling of that). I even laugh when I think of the day I got my hand caught in the door. We were heading to Roswell. I think about going to class after that and keeping my hand up to reduce the swelling the whole time looking like I was flexing a particular finger toward the professor. I remember Channel 7 and that time as so important in my life.

Not only did I feel welcomed, I adored everyone I worked with there. You always made me feel special in a way. I told you when I last was in Buffalo that working with you and working there taught me that I can really hold my own with the other professionals whom I would work with in the future. That semester I spent working for you was honestly one of the best times I ever had. I still have some of the pictures from that period of time as well... Including one of you in some kind of winter Russian type of hat.

I want to thank you for putting your trust in me. I want to thank you for teaching me so much. I want to thank you for being a friend, being a mentor and for being you. You are definitely one of the most wonderful people I ever had the good fortune to know. So if you ever doubt that you made a difference in someone's life (which I am sure you can already point to many many examples). You made a huge difference in my life. I only feel happy when I think of the time I got to spend with You and Frank and others. So thank you so much for being a light in my life.

Hi Kevin,

I have embarked on a personal project this week. I had Covid back in September. No one expected me to survive. I didn't expect to survive. One of the things I realized while in the hospital is that I was alright if this was going to be my end. I have been fortunate enough to live more in my one life than some people manage to do with two. The one thing I was saddened about though was that I wouldn't get to say goodbye to those who truly helped shape who I am today, and to thank them for their insight, trust, and mentorship.

After I survived Covid, I was left with a feeling of "What Now?" What do I do now. All the turmoil I ever experienced in my life including having melanoma in 2012 generally spurred me onto greater pursuits and more experiences. This time I was just left with an empty feeling really. That is why I am starting this project. Since the thing I was most saddened with was my lack of time to say things to the people who have helped me along the way, it's time to say those things to the people who helped me along my way.

Still to this day you are probably the best boss I ever had. You took a chance on me to start interning at WBEN with traffic control. I still have the drawing one of the other interns left for me before I went to college. I still have WBEN notepad paper. I have plenty of pictures and truly fond memories. But you still are the person I think of when I think of the best boss. I have had plenty of them, and I will never forget one of the things you said to me. After I had made a mistake, you calmly just said, you know you made the mistake, there is nothing that you could say because I already realized what I had done and you left it with that. That was so impressive and so well beyond the times.

Today I notice that people have degrees but they have no leadership skill or ability. They have no real knowledge about how to be a supervisor without being a jerk about it. You were way ahead of the ballgame.

I really was impressed as well when I started to look for a new job to further my career and you said it was okay to be looking. That you weren't going to hold it against me. So often I have had supervisors get mad and take revenge for me looking for new opportunities. Out of all the experiences I have been blessed to have, I know I need to attribute my start to you. You gave me a chance when I was just in high school. You welcomed me back after college. I just really have always appreciated that.

I tried to call you a couple of times when you started your own business to say congratulations. I could never catch you, and I assume you probably thought my area code might have been a spam call as well since it is a 307. I don't recall actually if I left a message. But late as it is, Congratulations on your business!!

The last couple of times I have been home in 2012 and 2015 I made stops at the new WBEN offices and got to see Sandy Beach before he retired, Tim Wenger and of course Tony who was always a fixture at the station. But I didn't get a chance to say hello to you. So I hope this letter finds you well. I just wanted to make sure you knew, how much I have always appreciated you and how you took a chance on me. How you truly were one of the great ones to work for.

I am coming home for my cousin's wedding if the weather works in February. I have asked Linda Pellegrino as well but I would love to say hello and maybe take you both to lunch on either the 9th or 10th of February. I know that is a long way out but since I am sending this I figured I would ask.

Thank you so much for being such a great mentor, you truly impacted my life and I wanted to make sure I got a chance to thank you for that.

Hi Phil,

I still remember the night I met you and your daughters (pre-Leah). I had just two snickers' bars left when I saw your kids and tried to lure them over to the patrol car as they stood on the sidewalk just looking at me. That will forever be a night that changed my life.

It is rare to find individuals who will take you in really and treat you like family, as you and the whole family did. I loved watching all four of your kids grow up, get older, and at least two now having kids and lives of their own now. Being able to be even a small part of that has been so special to me.

I remember the night we first really talked too, the night I was headed to the Arthur Center with a patient, and I sped through Kingdom City only to hear you call me on the radio and asked me to stop in at your office when I returned. I really did at that time think you were going to yell at me for speeding through that area. The night I was working in Texas County when you happened to drive by and stop at the gas station was really a wonderful surprise as well. It took me a couple of seconds to figure out why I knew the kids walking in the door!

I appreciate more than words can say how often you welcomed me into your home when I was in town. How often I could depend on you to be a sounding board when I needed. We don't do enough to tell people that made an impact in our lives just how much they did and that is why I am writing this letter. I probably would not have even been here anymore without you and your support and kindness. Thank you for putting your trust in me as well.

My life would never have been the same without that Halloween night. I do miss chatting with you more often, but I know you are busy trying to live your life and holding down basically two full time jobs. I always do think of you though and pray you are doing well. Thank you for all your impact in my life.

Hi Denise,

Remember when we were in St. Louis having that yummy delicious Chinese food? I remember talking to you quite a bit about having Covid and my life afterwards. I know I told you that I was at kind of a loss for what to do now. That I didn't have any particular goals or desires that I haven't already met.

I remember meeting you during the Citizen's Police Academy. Then shortly thereafter when I started working at Cracker Barrel. You became a true friend. When I had to leave that job you were so supportive and I really appreciated it. When I became a police officer and heard another officer run a plate that had your name attached to it, I realized that I would be able to find you again!! You again allowed me to be part of your life. You became a very good friend to me. I also appreciate how well you fit in with the people I worked with. Rich really did like you. I was so happy that you also reached out to me when you were running into trouble with Hampton.

When I reached a point in time in my life where I was struggling to actually survive, you and Pat were both there for me. When I managed to get off that particular medication that was causing my issues and I got my life back together again you were still there, so thank you so much. I don't know where I would have been without you. And even though I moved multiple times again, you are still there. Thank you for allowing me to be part of your life. We don't say it enough to the people we love, but I really do love you my friend. Without you my life would be very different and my life might not have been a life at all. I am still so sorry for completely knocking your neck out of alignment when I hit you with the racket ball. I need to pay you back for any medical bills!! I should have offered to sooner. Or maybe I will take you with me on a vacation in the future!

It is really one of the highlights of my trip to St. Louis each year that I get to see you and have some time to chat with you. I was so excited for you embarking on that new career like you did. Really proud of you too. You took a chance and it turned out in your favor. And yes I voted from Wyoming for you to be the best groomer in Columbia!! But more so overall, I just want to thank you for being my friend. It isn't always easy to find good people. You have meant the world to me and I just wanted you to know that. Thank you for everything you have done, and will do.

When you retire, I will have to take you on a trip somewhere.

Hi Sara,

I know I met you when you were still working at the WWCC computer lab. I am not overly clear on how we actually became friends. I have thought about this for a while. I can't really remember the day or the time or the incident that really drew us together as friends, but oh my gosh, I don't know how I would have survived without you.

So maybe you can fill me in on how we became friends, but I wanted to thank you for giving me a chance. I knew I was the new guy on campus and didn't know a soul in that town, without you and a couple others, I would have hit the road away from that place long before I actually did.

Thank you for all the invites to celebrate Thanksgiving and Christmas with your family especially since I had no where else to go. Thank you for all the kindness that I probably didn't always deserve. The way you helped me with melanoma and getting me to Salt Lake when I needed to get there. I don't think I ever really had a friend that would do so much for me.

I know the trip to Australia was a disaster and left you holding the bag to take care of the kitties when you shouldn't have had to, I am so sorry. I know the trip to get me to the airport was hard on you and I am so more than grateful for you.

Thank you for letting me part of your life, thank you for letting me be part of your family's lives, I really adore your mom and the whole group. I know I depended on you a lot and it probably wasn't all that fair to you but you were kind of a rock for me when I needed it. I will always remember the fun we had in cake decorating classes and the story of your sister sleep eating her bow.

You are such an amazing person and my life is better because I know you. You are loved dearly and I deeply appreciated everything you helped me with. I would have felt so bad if I had died and not gotten a chance to thank you and tell you just how wonderful you are.

We don't do this enough with the people we surround ourselves with. It was time to let you know just how important you are to me and how much you mean to me. Love you, and I hope I will be able to get back to Wyoming in the future and we can be old cake decorating biddies together:)

Hi Fr. Joe,

We actually have never met in person but you were always in my "section" of professional development when we all started teaching for Corinthian. I loved teaching for them. I enjoyed interacting with you in our development classes. You were always very entertaining. I knew you were the first one to call when I moved to Wyoming and needed new adjunct instructors. I knew you would say yes, and I am so happy I followed through and asked you because the students really liked you, as did the staff in the office.

You helped me out for the entire time I was out there I think. 13–14 years? I was so glad I had an adjunct I could trust to get things done and to give students great classes. I know I leaned on you a couple of times when things started to get bad at that college. I wish things had been different. I would have been happy to stay there for my entire career, but it just got too difficult emotionally. The college started to take every opportunity to make life difficult for everyone on campus which is why I started searching for a new place to go.

I am so sorry you were ceremoniously let go from the college as well. That was all because of me, and the individual (whom I will not even name) decided she knew better and just got rid of all my people and added people of her own. It wasn't fair but I appreciated that you took it in stride. I am so sorry they didn't treat you any better. And they should have.

The one thing I truly want to thank you for and tell you how much I appreciated you was your help with my friend Myron. Without question, you wrote him a recommendation letter to help him. I know you tried to talk to him while he was in jail sadly that system didn't work very well but I do know you tried and that meant so much to me. You wrote him that letter and then you offered to help him after he got out of jail. There was only so much I could do, but you really without question offered to help and that meant a lot to me.

When Myron left I was devastated, I had lost someone that was so close to me. It was a hard time and I knew you were there if I needed you.

Thank you, my friend, for everything you did for me. My life wouldn't have been the same without you. Thank you for the invites to your life Facebook sessions, I tried to attend a couple of times. Thank you for offering to help my friend even though you didn't know him. You took my word for it and went to bat for him for me. Thank you so much.

I truly hope one day we actually get to meet in person!!!! But I know you are out there and thank you for all your prayers and support. Love you my friend.

Dearest Janell,

You tell me the story occasionally of how we first met, when I had come to Wyoming before actually moving there, with a load of stuff in my car to drop off in the office so I didn't have as much to move come moving day about a month later. You ran by and grabbed the cart that was left for me. And you said you would be right back. I kind of have a memory of that, little did I know how much you would factor in my life after that. I know my first real interaction with you and Kit was a game night I believe. It was so nice of you all to include me in your plans, since I was there alone and didn't know a soul it really was an important thing for me to be invited.

When I think of some of the best times, I think about you and Kit, whether it was the rodeo or just going out to eat or to the movies. And the work you really did that one year to make my birthday a good one even though a blizzard stopped us in our tracks. The best though no doubt was the time we would spend at Half

Moon Lake with one another. Omg the laughter. I just can't imagine what life would have been without you. I am smiling now thinking about all those years we went up to that cabin. That game needs to be enshrined in the "best games ever" museum.

    I know you are going through a tough time right now and I hope this letter gives you a little bit of solace. I love you so much and thank you for including me in your family and everything. You are very special my friend. Life would never have been the same without you. My life was better because you were in it. I love you my friend and I will see you again one of these days, I promise.

Dearest Kit,

    I don't think I have ever had someone I would call a best friend since high school prior to you. I know I told you a little bit about the letters I was writing, so I won't go into too much detail as to why I am writing them. I just knew this was something that had Covid taken me away I would have liked to be able to say. I would have been sad had I left the world without getting to tell some very special people just how special they are.

    I don't remember the first time we met. I have a memory that might have been your birthday at your house and everyone was excited about a gift you had gotten from your boyfriend at the time, that seemed to indicate that we would have a wedding soon. I don't say this to make you sad, I just am sharing what I think is my first real memory of you after moving to Wyoming.

I do recall you coming across as this little sprite like leprechaun that had fairy dust sprinkling around everywhere you went. You were and are just so adorable. I know I have you to thank for making me part of your friend group. I didn't know anyone at the college and I didn't know anyone in town. I was there by myself and you were the one to start inviting me to places. Without you, I might not have stayed in Wyoming. Without you, I would have been so lonely.

When I left Wyoming, it was you that did all the stuff that made me feel so special. You helped me pack, you helped me when I was not doing well. You created a beautiful room out of my downstairs room when it was a complete disaster. You did it without asking for anything in return. I don't know many people who are so giving. I don't know many people who would do the things you have done for me without question.

Thank you is not enough. I owe you so much. There were times I didn't want to continue on and you were always there for me to lean on when I didn't think I could move forward.

The best memories with you though had to be the times we spent at half moon lake. Oh my gosh the time we had to spend together, the laughing we were able to do, the dang game that was just the funniest thing ever. That was probably one of the best times I have ever had.

Had I not survived Covid, I would have felt bad that I didn't get a chance to tell you just how amazing you are. I would have felt bad that I disappeared without letting you know I had to leave. You honestly are one of the best people I have probably ever had the honor to meet and to know. You just do everything you can to help everyone and you do it without any pay back. I didn't know just how lucky I was to meet you; I know now just how lucky I have been to be able to call you, my friend.

I still hope I can one day make it back out to Wyoming when I retire. I am not sure where the world is heading but I know I was lucky to know you have you be part of my life. Love you.

Hi Suzanne,

I remember meeting you sometime after arriving at Westminster, way back in August of 1988. Has it been that long? I really appreciated having some friends there on the hallway. I know that one night everything went to hell because I just wanted to be left alone. There is no way I should have allowed that incident to end our friendship. I was so glad that we got back together as friends eventually while we were still in school.

I think we were able to keep up an email friendship for a while after school, but ultimately, I think it was Facebook that we actually have to thank for being able to actually reconnect. I remember being in Vegas for a conference and learning for some reason that you happened to be in Las Vegas as well. We were able to meet up for dinner one night.

What I really appreciate was how willing you were to try to travel, so I could go places!! I wanted to go to a lot of places and I didn't really have anyone else I was friends with who were interested. I reached out to you and was so excited that you were game! Our first trip of course was Alaska and I totally missed you getting off the plane. From that point forward I have truly appreciated your willingness to travel with me. I truly have appreciated having you as a friend. You were always quick to ask if I needed anything after being in the hospital and that means a lot to me.

I hope you have enjoyed traveling as much as I have, even though checking in at times has been "interesting" to say the least. One time I was at the boat before you and of course the fateful New Zealand trip when we were a couple days late. I also really appreciated you welcoming my mom on that trip as well.

So overall what I want to say is, thank you for giving me a second chance. Thank you for being adventurous and willing to fly off to all kinds of places to just meet up and go on a cruise. You have truly been an awesome travel partner and here's to looking forward to next year. Of course, I have to update my passport now. I am sending these letters to people to thank them and I don't need any reply or response. We don't do these things enough really.

I realized when I started these letters that there were a lot of people I needed to thank. A lot of people I needed to say how much I have appreciated them giving me their friendship. Can't wait for Michigan this weekend, it isn't Paris, but we can have fun anywhere!!

Dearest Joe,

I wanted to get this letter to you before I saw you next week. I am not doing this to get responses. I am not doing this for anything other than my appreciation for them. We don't do this kind of thing enough; we don't tell people enough just how much they have meant in our lives. As for you...

I can't remember when we met. It must have been at an ILEETA but I have no idea which one it was, you just were one of those people that were always just there. Maybe you recall when we actually met, but knowing you has made all the difference.

I know you were helpful when I was still in Wyoming with a class. I know you were helpful in allowing me to take your classes to be able to have some continuing education which I am required to do for work. But you of course were always more than that to me. You nicely tolerated my "quirks" I guess. Sometimes people just don't like how outgoing I can be, or just how annoying I can be at times.

Of course when I was faced with a personal struggle dealing with Myron and trying to get him out of jail, trying to get him a lawyer, trying to prevent him from taking his life and you were there every step of the way and that means a lot to me. I don't have many friends here in Iowa and it isn't easy to open up to any of the ones I do here with my grief, but you were there when I needed you and there was no reason you had to be. There was no reason why you did what you could for me after Myron left, other than you being an amazing angel. I have always believed that certain people are put in our path to be there for certain events to help us make it through.

I still miss Myron, but without you I don't know if I could have survived it. So thank you for all you have done for me. Thank you for tolerating me, thank you for not abandoning me in times of need. You don't have to do what you have always done for me so please know that I more than appreciate it. You are an amazing person and I hope you know that. Thank you again for letting me call you a friend.

Hi Heather,

I remember meeting you for the first time. It was summer and I was there at the Sheriff's Dept and you were just hired to take over for Norma. You seemed very nice and I was right. Throughout the summer we really became friends and I definitely appreciated that. The next summers after that I really felt grateful to have you around. You seemed to have my back many times, especially in that mess with the A-hole I dated there, whose name will not be used. When I told you the story, you didn't judge me or at least you didn't seem to, and you really just seemed to understand where I was coming from and what really had happened.

I have appreciated your friendship all these years, I can't really even say which year we met, but I am so grateful we did. I appreciated you letting me know that Myron was having troubles, I might never have known had you not told me. I managed to write to him often and keep in touch with him during the last couple years of his life. Time I really would have missed if I didn't know. So, thank you for telling me. Thank you for letting me know that he had gone missing too. I knew it was close, I had spoken to him the week before on Facetime and I saw so much emotion in him, and then he told me he was going to Niagara Falls the next day. I knew he was having a hard time ending his life and figuring out how to do so. As soon as he told me where he was going, I knew that was the end for him.

I truly appreciated being able to lean on you a bit in our shared grief of losing our friend. I wish things could have been different but he was hurting so much that he just couldn't do it anymore.

We don't do things like this enough. We don't tell people just how much of a difference they have made in our lives. I want you to know that. I always know that you are out there, and thank you for being you. I wanted to make sure I took the time to let you know just how amazing you really are. Thank you for being a friend!

Hi Bryan,

I am writing this note to you because I wanted to say thank you.

You, I met online in class. I liked you online right away. It was fun to interact with you on the discussion board and then in email and eventually by phone. Thank you for even allowing me to be a part of your life for a period of time. I know at times I can be annoying and say the wrong thing, I think I am better now, but you were very nice to me and overlooked my shortcomings. I really appreciated you allowing me to travel out to Idaho, I had never been that far west and I really liked being out that way. I am sorry for all the stupid annoying things I did. But I still really appreciated how much of a friend you were.

I am so glad that I called you the day I was offered the job teaching in Wyoming. I wasn't sure about the move I wasn't sure I was ready for such a huge move again, away from everyone I knew. You got on my case and as I recall it, you almost yelled at me for not accepting the job right away. Thank you for that because it really was a great move for me. I spent 12 years in Wyoming and I really came to love living there and being with the friends I made out there. I was so sad to leave that college but it had become a difficult place to work. So, I had to move on, but boy do I miss being out in the Rockies. I will have to try to go back one day.

    I just wanted to make sure I sent you this note to let you know just how much I appreciate you, what an amazing person you are, how welcomed I felt when I visited with you allowing me to spend time even with your family and how honored I am to be able to say you are a friend. Thank you for making me feel welcome. You should know how much I admire you and appreciate all the things you helped me with. Thank you for everything my friend. I am glad I got an opportunity to follow through on the one thing I thought about when I was nearing death's door.

    Thank you for everything!

Dear Cindy,

    I met you at some point after I got to Western. I can't really even remember when or which day or how or anything. I know I was so excited to be somewhere that had a pool that I could use. So I assume I met you surrounding that activity. I am so grateful that we became friends.

    I was in Wyoming all alone and only a few people welcomed me into their life and even into their family. Thank you so much for giving me a part time mom while I was there with you mother. Thank you for being a sounding board when I needed it. Thank you for allowing me to go to SLC with you and your mom on many many occasions. Or even when you just picked up water for me. Thank you for allowing me to hang with you at the cabin those few weekends! You were truly a great friend. And I know distance has gotten in the way of daily or even weekly conversation, I think about you a lot. I miss being able to swim with you and that pool. OMG loved that pool. The pool I have here is only 4ft deep, only 3 lanes wide and it is a meter pool so it is shorter than what I am used to. I miss your pool.

But most of all, I miss you Cindy. You were always someone I could depend on. I am sure there were times I made you mad or caused you aggravation. But you always gave me a second chance. So thank you for that. Thank you for being my friend, Thank you for sharing your family with me and thank you for being you. My life out there wouldn't have been the same without you. You really are a great person and you should know that.

I would have been sad had I not had the opportunity to tell you these things. I appreciate you and love you so much. I wish I didn't have to be separated from all my friends out there. I do hope to come back out there one day. But I wanted to make sure that you knew, I didn't take you or anything you helped me do for granted. I appreciated everything you did for me.

I miss you walking up and down the hall in your sometimes strange outfits, like the yellow cap on your head one day. I seem to remember other "outfits" as well. You were always such a joy to see and talk to. Thank you so much for everything.

Dear Janine,

    I don't remember when we met, I know I was probably only three or four but you were my first real friend and my best friend all through the first years of my life. When I moved we definitely drifted apart as that is what usually happens in life, but there are memories that I always remember. Trying to run by the house of your next door neighbor so he wouldn't see me and call me carrot top. What was his name? Mr. Farley? The times we made tents and slept in the back yard. The time we traveled to Rochester to compete in that first dance competition.
    I remember playing for hours on end with you and your brother in your pool and then in ours after we got it. Dance class and the purple people eater. You are basically what I remember when I think about my early childhood. So, thank you for being my friend, thank you for being part of my story.
    I still occasionally think about some of the sad times too especially that one day we were going to get our notes in to walk to school and home, and you ran back in to get your note and the bus came and I didn't know what to do. I still feel bad about that and I am so sorry. I should have waited and walked with you. Overall though I hope you look back and think of that time of life with a smile and with fond memories. I just wanted to thank you for being my childhood really. I hope you're doing well, and enjoy-

ing being a grandmother now!!! Gosh can we be that old?

My Dearest Angela,

I met you the first time when you arrived for an interview, and I had to ask if your hair was naturally curly. I was happy to welcome you into my home for your first month or so of working at—the place not to be named anymore. Not only because you did my dishes, but because I got to know you really well. I was so proud to be called your friend. I so appreciated all your enthusiasm and the fun that we got to have.

So thank you for being my friend, thank you for putting your trust in me, thank you for being part of my life, it just wouldn't have been the same without you. I wish we didn't have to be so far apart now, and I hope your future does involve a move both you and RJ want to make you happy. Thank you for being my friend and being there for me when I needed a shoulder or an ear. You are amazing and I can't wait to see where your future takes you!!

To all of my former, current and future students,

In the last 15 years I have watched so many of you grow up, get married, have kids, accomplish goals, and overall just kicking butt in the world and it truly makes me smile for having just a little part of your story.

It has been my honor to have been part of your lives. So I want you all to know just how much I have appreciated every one of you.

I have all of you to thank for making my life truly wonderful. There are so many of you I would find it hard to mention you all, but just know that I have been so very very proud of each and every one of you for going out there and doing good things. Going out there and becoming who you are today. I have also been impressed with how much you are all accomplishing in this world. I have truly enjoyed watching you grow through your pictures on Facebook and so many of you adding to your family. It makes my heart happy to see just how many of you are out there doing this thing called life—so well!!

So thank you for letting me be a part of your life, it has been my honor, it has made me so happy to see you all doing so well. I am so glad I got this opportunity to tell you how I feel. I would have missed out had I not survived. Always know that I am around for you, please continue to share the great things you do with me through either Facebook or some other way. I am so proud of all of you, thank you for letting me be part of your story.

Dear Mike, and Tracy

I met you when I started working during the summers for the Sheriff's Department. You were always very nice to work with and then I got the chance to work directly with you when you moved over to the SO. It was a joy to be able to work with you. I really appreciated the knowledge you shared, the friendship you provided and how much you made me feel like part of the team.

> You were a great partner and I loved working every second with you. I wanted to thank you for making me feel like family. You are Tracy. You two are so special and I will never forget how you made me feel. Thank you for everything.

I wasn't sending the letters expecting a reply. The letter-writing was not an ego exercise. I just realized throughout my time on this earth and how things have changed so much that we are more and more lonely, we don't get a chance to have personal conversations opting instead for texting. By the time I was old enough to really look at and realize the amazing help my heroes gave to me we had already gotten to the point where we were getting further and further away because technology was starting to take the place of the phone call, the handwritten letter, or the one-on-one conversation.

I've always said thank-you to people as I left for a future opportunity or when the job was done, but in this day and age of people being so distant, now was the time to make that change. I almost didn't get the chance. I would like to think that maybe this is something that everyone should consider. In the world today of being so disconnected physically, maybe it is time to make that connection.

I did get many responses though, each and every one of them healing my heart. Each and every one of them made me truly believe that I had a big impact on people, and they will have impacts on others. One of my favorite TV shows was the original *Quantum Leap*. In the final episode of that series, Sam was told that he's "done a lot of good in this world" and told that he "could still do so much more." With the letter project, I felt just like Sam; I now knew that I had done a lot of good in this world and maybe I could still do much more.

Some of the responses I received lifted my heart:

> I am so glad to hear you survived something like that. I don't think I ever would have joined corrections if it weren't for your classes. If I hadn't, I never would have met my husband.

I genuinely enjoyed the classes I took with you more than any other classes I took throughout the years for my Bachelor's Degree. Thank you for putting a realistic but fun spin into teaching and Criminal Justice. I owe much of my success and meeting my wonderful husband to you. Thank you for reaching out! I hope you are doing much better now (Tori)

Love you so much Traci and I am so blessed to have had you as my professor at Hawkeye. I actually was thinking about reaching out to you because I haven't heard from you for a while and I was starting to get worried. I also know you don't post much on Facebook either so thought maybe you don't put that much out there. I appreciate you for reaching out and I am so sorry to hear about your illness. I am so glad you survived Covid because you will always be considered a dear friend of mine. Let me know if you ever need anything, I'm just a message or a call away. XOXO (Alexis)

Thank you so much! I have searched multiple times seeing how you have been doing and I haven't seen much!!! Know I'd love to stay in thought and I'd be happy to hear from you on occasion. I am now dispatching and have for the past 6 months. I appreciate you believing in me! And I am so glad to hear from you, and I hope you are doing good now!!! Love to you!!!! (Chantell)

OMGOSH Traci, as I sit here with tears streaming down my face I just love you!!! I'm so sorry you had to go through what you do!!! I lost my dad to Covid in October and my heart still breaks. You are a strong individual and I'm so grateful to have you in my life. Take care of yourself and I'm always here!! (Tia)

I am so pleased to read this. I am so happy to hear you beat Covid. It's a nasty virus. Traci, you truly impacted my life. Helped me achieve my goals. You inspired me and still do. You helped give me the nudge to go chase my dreams before even finishing my degree. Thanks for reaching out. I'm sorry to hear Covid hit you so hard. I've been thinking of you often not seeing any news posts had me wondering. Hugs and stay safe my friend (Shell)

Love you Traci!! Thank you for being an inspiration. Your teaching is incredible and has such an impact. (Stevie)

Thank you for that. It was a king read but very heartfelt and I am blessed you were my professor and my friend. I am very glad you didn't give up and that you're still among us. It means a lot that you took the time to send this out to me and others that you have thought about over the years. Please stay in touch and don't be afraid to let us know what is going on in your life. I'd had to lose another friend. (Ryan)

Thank you for everything Traci!!! Going to Hawkeye was the best decision I made so far. I met lifelong friends and I felt like all the professors really wanted me to succeed. You always pushed me to do my best and always supported my goals. I can't wait to see what my future has in store for me and I will for sure keep you in the loop. Thank you Traci!! (Thom)

I am so sorry that I didn't know how sick you were. Words cannot express how happy I am that you survived and while we don't get to connect often, I think of you a lot. You've made such a huge impact on my life and genuinely feel I would not be where I am today without the love, support and guidance I received from you. You were there for me in ways far beyond a teacher or even a mentor, encouraging me to do the scary things and helping me with personal issues that you could have easily brushed to the side and not discussed with me at all. The best part, it always felt genuine and I always felt nothing but love and support from you. Moving to Boston was a life changing decision for me and you 1000% supported that decision. The only person in my life that did that at the time. In fact, I am forever grateful for everything you've done for me, for always being the best sounding board, pushing me to be great when I doubted myself and for helping me become the woman that I am. Thank you for being a HUGE part of my life/story. I love you!! (Samantha)

I'm so sorry to hear about your struggle last September, I wasn't aware but I'm so glad you recovered! And I need to thank you for also having such an amazing impact on my life! In your class and with all the opportunities you gave me I was able to grow as a person. I gained confidence in myself in many ways that I can't even begin to explain. You showed me ways to stand up for myself through the confidence I found! I learned a lot in your classes and it wasn't just criminal justice (although I find that information so helpful in my life as well!) And you were always so kind to me! So thank you for being so wonderful! Easily one of the best teachers I've ever had! Thank you for being in my life! (Megan)

It's so good to hear from you Traci. I still think about your classes and am grateful for the experiences I had. I don't think I would be where I am today without your guidance. I am glad you are doing better and I hope things continue to go well for you! (Taylor)

Traci, you have been not only an amazing teacher/professor towards me but you went out of your way to take care of me when I was struggling in school. You took me out to eat and to teach me shoot. These days people are so greedy and don't care for anyone but them selves. You don't just give a part of yourself, when you care you give ALL of yourself to make sure the other person is okay. You made school fun and have taught me so many things. You're an amazing friend and I'm blessed to have you in my life. I'd still like to go to our diner place and get lunch or dinner some time. Our conversations are not just the best mentors but some that I'd like to confuse to create. You're a blessing on the earth and I'm so lucky that I have gotten the chance to be a part of you. If you're still up for lunch or dinner I would be more than happy to pick you up and take us out. You're a big blessing Traci, thank you ♥ (Marijana)

Awe Traci! Thank you! You will always be one of my most favorite instructors and that blue blanket you got me for graduation remains a staple on my bed. You taught me to look at things from a different perspective which has helped me throughout my career and life. I'm very thankful you are better. (Karen)

I'm so happy to hear you are healthy again. I only had one or two classes with you, but they were my favorite. I learned so much from your classes and enjoyed them immensely. You are an amazing teacher. I just recently passed my 5 year mark with the WDOC. I feel like everything I learned from you gave me a good jump start into my career. I will always cherish the lessons from you and hope you live much longer to influence many more students to come. Thank you so much Traci!!! (Alex)

Oh my goodness Traci! I didn't have any idea, but I did mention to Juanita and I hadn't seen much if any activity on here for quite some time. I am so glad you are ok! I am sorry I wasn't closer or I would have done what I could to lend a hand while you were fighting and recovering. What a story and a great reminder, as we have seen in the last couple of years especially, that what really matters like the relationships with others around us and just how well we treat each other. That reflects in the memories we look back on and can smile and recall fondly. 🖤 (Jennifer)

Oooof, I read all of this with tears in my eyes because I don't know that you fully know the impact you've had and continue to have on my life. You are an incredible human being; so selfless and willing to move mountains for your students. I never knew my love of law enforcement before you. And to appreciate and experience life to its fullest. I'm so sorry to hear about your health issues and I hope you are recovering and overcoming them. Please come out to Virginia! My wife and I would love to have you. Love you and most of all thank you, from the bottom of my heart for being my mentor, confidant and advisor (Whitney)

Traci—This past year has been a roll coaster of excitement and hardships. I started my new career that I have worked for, for a long time now. I have become a husband, recently I have become a father, with my future son expected in October. I bought a house, I have debt. And so much more. This roller coaster of events started with the completion of my education at Hawkeye. Only a little over a month after graduation I was starting my new career. I am one of the youngest cops to ever have been hired by my department and I am the youngest full time road cop In the entire county. Just a few days ago I had my 1 year anniversary of working for Oelwein. It's been a blast, I have started to find my groove, I have experienced a wide variety of calls and my work has been being noticed. This doesn't mean that this job hasn't been hard. As I reflect on this past year there has been many things I have done and seen that most people will never do or see in their entire live times. Now, for some things this can be cool, like driving fast, playing with cool gadgets, working with firearms and so much more cool things that we see and do. However, as you know, this job also has its dark side. We see some pretty tough things that to others, would be the worst thing they have ever seen and the worst thing they probably will ever see. However, we push through and continue on. We see dark things on a regular basis. That's why I appreciate how much you and other instructors talked about it. Taking care of ourselves and our brothers and sisters in blue is top priority. I now see why you guys emphasize that soo much. Not only do us in law enforcement need our partners to get through hard times but we also need you. We need people like you who were in our shoes and now are preparing us for this career. Your job is not easy. Trying to prepare 18 and 19 year old kids for the life of a cop isn't easy. However, let me ensure you that you have done an amazing job. What I learned from you and others is the reason I'm the cop I am today. I use the knowledge and insight you have passed down to do my job to the highest ability possible out of me. I honestly would not be as confident and possibly not even in the same career if it wasn't for the wisdom you had passed down to me and so many other students. Sometimes I am sure that your job might feel unimportant and that students don't appreciate it. I am here to tell you that even if you don't hear it enough, your job is crucial to the success and longevity of this profession and the ones like me who are filling the positions within it. We need you, and we need your guidance, wisdom and insight. I have nothing but good to say about Police Science. I have recommended it to so many kids I have talked to who are interested in law enforcement. You guys truly care about us as students. You don't just see us as another class. You see us as individuals and care about us individually. You care about our success in this career not only intellectually but also our longevity and our health and happiness in this career. It's a big task. But I'm proof to show that the work you are putting in, going the extra mile for students, truly does have an impact and it makes a huge difference in our career. Just the other day I was talking about Hawkeye with some of my cop buddies. One guy talked about how he teaches a class at University of Upper Iowa. I spoke highly of Hawkeye and I said if I ever got the opportunity to help out, I would love to give back to the program and help teach students, my future partners, at Hawkeye Police Science/CJ. On a personal note. I want to say thank you for personally being there for me. I know I shared some personal things with you when I was having a hard time and you were there for me to lift me up. When I felt like giving up, you were a big reason I pushed on. And now, I couldn't be happier with my decision to keep pushing on. Much of my success is credited to your wisdom and knowledge you passed down. It meant a lot to me that even though every year you have 50–100 new students. You still took the time to talk to me and care about my success individually. Everything you did for me means a lot to me. I greatly appreciate you and I am glad you pushed through your illness and was there for me. When you ask yourself what now? I say, the reason you are still here is for people like me. We need you, we need your guidance, we need your help. If we are going to grow to become great cops, in every aspect. We need you! Thank You for everything! I am looking forward to my career and my family's growth and I am grateful that I had someone like you to prepare me for this career. Like I said I would love to give back to the program one day and help out. Keep me in mind if you ever need someone for the program. Keep doing the good work of preparing us to be successful. You mean a lot to soo many of us! We all love you as well (Codi)

Hey Traci, JodiRae here messaging on my mom's phone real fast. That's one thing I do miss about Facebook is keeping in touch with folks. Anyway, I can't put into words what this message did for me—especially the chaos of life lately, I needed it, and it coming from you was a sign from God to keep pushing. First of all, I had no idea you were sick. I'm glad to hear you made it through. I can't imagine going through all of that, but you're a badass Traci… there's nothing you can't get through. Secondly, thanks for reaching out. There is so much more I need to overcome and wish to accomplish, but you're also one of the first people I think of when I think about wanting to make someone proud. I was a naive 18 year old college freshman when you came into my life, and man you've had an impact since then. There's so much I've learned from you and so many ways you've helped me grow as an individual—not just with school either, but everyday life. I miss you at Western and it'll never be the same without you there teaching. Thanks for pushing me. I promise you, I'm gonna get that degree some day. Thanks for the constant inspiration, and just know how special you've been in my eyes since day one. So good hearing from you, and again, I'm glad you pulled through. Best wishes and continue to stay in touch! ♥ (JodiRae)

I am so glad to hear you survived something like that. I don't think I ever would have joined corrections if it weren't for your classes. If I hadn't, I never would have met my husband! I genuinely enjoyed the classes I took with you more than any other classes I took throughout the years for my Bachelor's Degree. Thank you for putting a realistic but fun spin into teaching and Criminal Justice. I owe much of my success and meeting my wonderful husband to you. Thank you for reaching out! I hope you are doing much better now! (Tori)

Wow, I am so glad that you survived and are doing better. I will always remember my time at Western with you! Feels like so long ago, but it wasn't really. Take really good care of you! 🐶 (Autumn)

Hey Traci! Wow reading your heart felt message just gave me chills and a tear to my eye because I didn't know what you were going through. I am so grateful I received this message and I'm honored that I was able to make an impact in your life that you have remembered me! A little update in my life. I have lived in Utah for 5 years. I graduated from Weber State and I'm currently working for the University of Utah. I also just bought a house down here!! (I know crazy right?!) anyways my life is pretty simple. With all the events and struggles going on, I (we) keep moving forward. I just wanted to say thank you once again and that I'm so blessed and honored! I hope you are doing better or that I at least can continue to put a smile from cheek to cheek on you! Love you!! (Edgar)

I have been so blessed to have known you and been taught by you! I still talk about you all the time and all the memories we made those years! I'll never be able to repay the lessons not only in the class room but life that you taught all of us! I'm a better person for having known you! I'm so glad you're okay and still here with us today! This world is not ready to lose Traci! 🖤🖤 (Ashley G.)

I'm so sorry to hear all that. I'm so glad you survived. I was just thinking about you the other day. I finally graduated in May with my associates. Thank you for all you did while I was at wwcc. You were always my favorite teacher!! Love you! (Kiera)

Awww thank you Traci! You were definitely one of my favorite instructors and educators in general! I'm so sorry to hear how badly COVID affected you, like many others, and I'm so glad you managed to beat it even if it had to be by the skin of your teeth! (Kassi)

Thank you so much Traci for being a part of my life! Time in your classes are some of the greatest memories I have from college and life. I owe it to you for really driving my love for criminal justice. I have now been working as a deputy in corrections here in Utah for two years and I think about your classes a lot in my career. I should be the one telling you thank you because I'm not sure where I would be in life had it not been for your support in school and in athletics. You made the journey through college so easy and enjoyable. Love you right back and thanks for everything you've done for me! (Wade)

Omggg I love you my dear friend...and amazing professor...it is because of you I am where I'm at today... Father God please wrap your loving and healing arms around Traci and give her the strength and comfort of your love to help her heal. In Jesus name 🙏 Amen (Jennifer M.)

Thank you for your kind words Traci! I'm glad you are doing much better and thank you on the updates. You were one of the best instructors I have had in school and I couldn't have done it without your help. I officially graduated with my bachelors of applied science degree from UNI this past May and I'm in the process of getting a police job somewhere. I just re-enlisted in the air national guard! Everything is going well and I hope you are doing good now too! (Matt)

I am so sorry to hear that you have been sick, I'm glad that you had the chance to tell your stork. You are such an incredible person, and you are loved by many! Traci, you were my first criminal justice professor, and I loved being in class with you, hearing about all your stories as a cop, and just life experiences in general. I personally have learned so much from you. Next semester will be my last semester at Southern Utah university. I will have my bachelors degree in criminal justice, and family relations. I am pleased to announce that I have started the process with Utah Highway Patrol, if all goes well I will be in the Academy in January 2023! (Jacob)

Traci—thank you for all of this, it was truly beautiful and you have been such a dear friend and peer. It is so odd that we have this powerful "virtual" reality that now because of Covid the world knows all too well. It does in fact work. I have to thank you more for everything you did for me—my time at WY was wonderful—but you were the best part of that—than the students—but as you have said so well. We both have been able to do so much…and this is a time to pause—to reflect—to HEAL (in many ways) so don't rush that. I still feel I could have done more for Myron, the 3 of us all know real pain and how harsh the system can be… I wish I could have gotten through, and those demons weren't so powerful. But that is the lesson learned, to keep going, keep fighting for justice, and not to let go. The new chapter will open soon and knowing you, it will be so exciting…we have been long over due for a face to face, for dinner, and that will happen… THANK YOU for this, it truly made my day! Love and blessings dear friend, Joe (Father Joe)

Traci, I am so happy you are okay! I know that we have had some wonderful times and I am thankful for you!! I miss some of the things that we did!! I have a few things to tell you that I probably should have already. I left Terry in October and started living in my own place. That is the first shocker… Then I started watching these girls for a guy and that gave me a little more freedom financially from Terry. Well I actually got a job running an RV park and Terry and I are still married for now. I have been living in my RV running this park. It has been hard and crazy, but I love it so far. The park manager is moving out of the house here so soon I will have my own house. I think that everyone will come live with me. Even Terry, but not as my mate. Only as my friend. So now I have since joined the investors in the park so I am part owner and so is Terry because we are still married. However I will be getting divorced and I think I have been waiting for Terry to accept this. I just can't be with him anymore...that too is a long story. So the park is in Jamestown and it is great! We still have the cleaning company and so it's hard to stop and tell you what has been going on because it's so much. Just know you will forever be my friend! Love you! Sara Now come see me (Sara N.)

Hello, Traci. I cannot begin to tell you how meaningful your message is to me. I have very fond memories of the people I worked with at WBEN and the times we all spent together, and you are among the people who helped to make it an experience the I cherish to this day. I have always tried to be nice to people. It's easier than the alternative! I sure would like to get together with you for when you are next in Buffalo so please keep in touch. I'm not sure if you know, but Bill Lacy is retiring from WHTT-FM. His last day, I believe, is Friday, May 27. It will be the end of an era and morning radio in Buffalo will never be the same. We still talk often and are playing golf this Saturday. Be well. I'm looking forward to reconnecting! (Kevin K.)

Traci! I have such fond memories of you and I loved this letter. I'm so grateful! You forgot one memory haha. I clearly remember you writing people's mistakes on your arm. And you were always right!! I would secretly laugh every time haha. I enjoyed every moment we shared and will always remember you and I'm so glad you are feeling better. What a scare! (Mary Alice)

5

The Vaccine

I always planned to take the vaccine. I never really planned to not take it, I happened to get sick before I did. Some of my coworkers got the vaccine when it first came out, some didn't, and some still haven't. I just wanted some time to make sure it was something I wanted to do.

I was planning to go on a cruise in 2022 and getting the vaccine was going to be required at least that was the current demand of the cruise line they were only following the required rules from the CDC. I knew if I was going to take the trip, I was going to have to get the vaccine. The vaccine combination had to be given with a certain amount of time in between I made sure that I scheduled it soon enough to be able to get both initial doses before the cruise was to start. I was required to have two of the original series and then one booster. I timed it specifically to be able to take that booster just a couple of weeks before boarding the boat.

I didn't want to get the vaccine when it initially came out. I admit I was nervous about it. I don't always react very well to medications. I am allergic to aerosol scents; I can't use clothing detergent that has any dye or perfume to it because I am allergic to it all. I was afraid that there might be something in the vaccine that I would be allergic to and once it was in, it wasn't going to ever come back out. What if I was allergic to it? How would that be treated? Would I just suffocate from anaphylaxis and then everything I went through having COVID would have been for nothing?

I also will admit, I was afraid. I was really concerned. I really wanted to wait a little bit to see how the vaccine was going over with people. How did it work if it was going to work? Were there any problems with it if there were? I just wanted some time to see what happened as people started to get the vaccine.

It was still something that is more experimental than not. I started to hear of people dying from heart issues that developed basically after they took the vaccine. I started to hear of other side effects as well. I started to hear that people were suffering from a Bell's palsy to one side of their face. I heard some other mumblings of side effects.

Unfortunately, because the social media outlets were restricting and censoring anything that was negative about the vaccines, I didn't hear everything I needed to. I don't have cable TV, and I generally just stream today so watching any real news was not in the cards. Not that the news was covering any of the negative aspects either.

Everything I did hear just played into my fear. I didn't want to get that vaccine. I already had COVID. I survived it. Doesn't that mean I have immunity, at least some? Does the cruise line really have to require these shots so I can take this trip? They can't go against the CDC and make a decision for themselves?

My time was running out, and I was going to have to make the decision, was I going to take the vaccine or give up the ability to travel, potentially ever again? It was already pretty clear the cruise line wasn't very willing to engage in discussions about getting my money back, so I felt pressured. The cruise line wasn't the only pressure.

There was a lot of pressure from my workplace to get the shot. If I didn't get the shot, then I would be required to wear a mask in perpetuity. The pressure from acquaintances was also pretty tough on me. I didn't know many people where I live, and it seemed individuals were avoiding me because I hadn't yet gotten the shot. It was already shocking to me how many people seemed to blame me for getting sick and not having the shot beforehand. I just didn't want to see it in people's faces anymore or hear in in their voices. The disappointment was just a little too much to handle.

With tears in my eyes, I got the first shot of the two-shot series. Then three weeks later, I got the second one. The only thing I experienced after the first shot was the flu like aches and pains I did hear about as being normal, so I didn't feel as if I needed to be worried about the second in the series.

It was December, right before Christmas when I was scheduled for the second shot. I again felt panic and tears in my eyes as the nurse drew the vaccine from the bottle. I watched as the second shot was administered to my left arm. I didn't know my life would never be the same again.

I was just about to leave after that second dose. When I remembered that I needed proof of the vaccine for my employer who was basically requiring that we provide proof. We were even instructed to submit the proof to a federal database and in return they would send us a card to show our vaccine status. Even though I submitted the proof I never could find a picture that suited their needs, so I never received my card.

I also needed the proof for the cruise line and probably the airlines. Either way, I asked the nurse quickly if she could print off the record for me.

As I waited in the lobby for that piece of paper, I felt strange. It hadn't been more than five minutes, but suddenly I felt very weak. I felt as if my legs were going to give out. I sat down just in case. I immediately thought to myself that I need to just suck it up. I was psyching myself out. I was just expecting something to go wrong so I must be experiencing a self-fulfilling prophecy. I pushed myself to just ignore the problem. I got my proof from the nurse, and I headed out of the office to my car.

I felt as if I was walking through mud and struggling to do so. I again tried to rationalize that nothing was wrong; it was just cold and windy out, so nothing was wrong I was just reacting to the weather. My plan that day was to go from the doctor's office to the gym. After COVID, I had worked really hard to get back some semblance of physical strength and aerobic capacity.

Before COVID, I was capable of biking about an hour, moving to walking and adding in a little bit of jogging before moving to the pool and swimming a mile. That would require thirty-five laps of the small pool in that gym. After COVID, when I felt well enough to get back into the pool, I was only capable of two laps. That was it; my capability of going any further was gone. I was having difficulty breathing, but my physical capability was also shot. I focused on swimming first as that tends to be my strongest event. I worked for weeks to get just a couple more laps each time. I finally made it to a mile, and then I started adding biking back in.

I had done well in the three months after COVID. Not only had I now managed to get back to being able to swim a mile in the pool but, I was also up to biking forty-five minutes. I even was able to walk about a mile. Now this was not all in the same day, which is what I was used to, but I was working on it. I was determined to get back to my old self. Sadly, that will never happen.

My plan for the gym that day was to walk a mile and then try to swim at least half of a mile to start combining workouts. What happened was anything but what my plan was. I started to walk the track at the gym. The track is one-sixth of a mile long. I wanted to try to walk seven laps and then move to the pool. I had a problem. I only made it about halfway around the track on lap 1, and my legs gave out. I couldn't move. I couldn't walk. I thought that maybe I was having an off day, and maybe I should just head home and try again tomorrow.

I had to use the railing on the track to support myself as I tried to get back to my bag. I struggled to get to my car. My legs weren't working; there was a strange pain that I hadn't felt before either. I got home that day and struggled the rest of the day to walk or to just get up from a sitting position. The next day, I was in store for more surprises.

The next day, I woke up and headed into my bathroom. I suddenly felt as if there was some kind of liquid on my arm. There was no water running; there was nothing dripping from the ceiling so what was it? Then it started to burn. I grabbed a washcloth to wipe off whatever the substance was. But it was too late; there was an obvious burn mark on my arm where the liquid had been. This was the same arm the injection went into the day before.

I tried to wash off my arm, and I was shocked at the fact that water mixed with whatever was on my arm burned as well. I suddenly flashed to the scene in that *Hunger Games* movie where the water healed the participants from the fog burn. I was experiencing the exact opposite. Later that day, I also noticed I itched. My underarm was on fire, and I needed to scratch it every few minutes. I headed to a mirror only to discover a massive red swollen rash throughout my entire underarm. A rash I had never experienced before. I have eczema but most of the time the rash shows up on my chest or on my hands. This was a new place I started to use the prescription eczema cream I have; the rash only spread wider and hurt more. Within a couple of days, the rash spread to my other underarm. My doctor didn't have any idea what it might have been. My dermatologist wasn't sure either, but I had another prescription cream given to me which at least took away the burning. The rash lasted for months. It occasionally still returns today. Once the rash showed up covering my entire left shoulder and part of my arm. Then more rash showed up on my right ankle. The rash is always the same, red, hot, burning, painful, and even with treatment with the prescription cream, it takes a long time to subside.

On the second day after the second vaccine, I went back to the gym and got onto a spin bike. It wasn't three days earlier that I had managed to bike for forty-five minutes. I was in tears within five, and I couldn't go anymore. My legs just didn't want to work. One day not being able to work out and walk, I can understand, maybe I just wasn't on my game that day. But two days in a row right after the vaccine, and my legs aren't working? It doesn't make sense.

As days went on, my performance didn't get better. I even tried to work with a trainer for a while. My ability to walk got worse and worse the more I tried to work with the trainer. I could lift weights. I could still swim, I just couldn't bike or walk. Swimming requires more upper body strength, which I still seemed to have although, I started to notice my swimming suffered.

Every day I was swimming less and less. I went from a mile to three-fourth of a mile to just a half. I started to notice if I worked out one day, I could barely get out of bed the next. I needed more and more sleep. If I swam on Saturday I could barely get out of bed on Sunday, and Monday was a huge struggle. This went on and on as I kept trying to keep up, it just became impossible.

When I got the second vaccine, I didn't want to blame the vaccine for the symptoms I was experiencing originally, but there was nothing else to point to. I had recovered from COVID. I do not have long COVID. I lost my physical capabilities the day of that second vaccine. Nothing else in my life was different. There was nothing else I could point to.

To add insult to injury, my cruise line did a very nice thing and decided to house some of the Ukrainian refugees from the war. The sad thing was they picked the boat I was supposed to cruise on in a few months. I was promised that the refugees would be off the ship before my cruise was to start. Three months later, I was rebooking my cruise for another year.

The cruise I took the vaccine for was cancelled. It might have been a selfish reason, but I wanted to go on the trip and so I sat for a vaccine I knew was going to be bad. Now my cruise was cancelled, and by the time the next opportunity rolled around, the vaccine was no longer required. I destroyed my life when I didn't have to. I couldn't have known the vaccine would eventually not be required, but I still blame myself for my situation. I sat for that vaccine when I shouldn't have all because I wanted to go on that trip.

As time went on, it was very clear that my left leg failed to work more often than the right. I noticed that occasionally, the leg seemed to be bigger than my right leg. The pain in my leg just never seemed to go away. The only thing I could point to as the cause was the vaccine.

There was no information available out there for the most part on those who experienced side effects. I had heard of some people dealing with Bell's palsy. The stories of athletes suddenly dying on the field started to make the news. The information about the heart problems experienced by young men who took the vaccine started to be covered in the media, but I really didn't hear much as to the things I was experiencing. I was a middle-aged female who was unable to walk. It wasn't Bell's palsy, and it wasn't myocarditis.

Then there was an actress who announced she was suffering from Guillain-Barre syndrome. Although the actress's case was not publicly related to anything, and it eventually disappeared from the news I started to do a little research into what this syndrome actually was. The symptoms seemed to fit. Although I wasn't immediately on that bandwagon, I continued to do research. Looking for answers.

I ended up watching a couple interviews through the Epoch News Service. Finally, someone was describing the side effects she had immediately ironically enough to the left side of her body the day she got the second vaccine. I started to learn about individuals who have lost the ability to move, individuals who have experienced nonstop pain—all this, of course, not covered in the major media outlets. I learned of suicides by individuals experiencing similar things to my symptoms.

I wanted to be honest in this book. And to be honest, it has been very difficult from going from an active triathlete, biker, swimmer to barely being able to get out of bed. The sudden disappearance of my typical exercise routine combined with the actual physical pain and loss of any of my actual capabilities—the depression is real.

I started to completely regret calling 911 the morning I was dying from COVID. I was almost there, if I had just rolled over that morning and went back to sleep, none of this would be going on. I wouldn't have ever taken the vaccine. I wouldn't be experiencing this pain. I wouldn't have lost all my ability to be active. I could have just drifted away in my bed that morning. I should have died. The depression is real. I would cry every morning just trying to get out of bed. I would tear up every day after coming home from working, knowing how exhausted I was.

I was afraid to sit on my couch, knowing I was going to have to struggle to get back up. I didn't feel like I could control my body anymore. I started to experience pain in my left shoulder as well. Every time I had to type on my computer, which has been in the same place for the last three years caused pain in my left shoulder.

My left side has obviously been impacted much more than my right. My lower body extremities are also more impacted than the top half of my body. I started to participate in water aerobics classes because that was all I seemed to be capable of anymore, lap swimming just dried up.

When I spoke to my regular doctor about how my legs and in particular my left leg just wouldn't work anymore, all she could offer me was physical therapy. I had just finished working with the physical trainer and discovered that my physical capability continued to decrease; what is a physical therapist going to do? At this point, I resigned myself to simply trying to navigate this new situation. I tried to figure out how to exist in a state of pain and disability.

I wasn't really sure how I was going to navigate this new world. What I did know is that my ability to handle all these things wasn't really up to the task. The nothingness feeling after COVID was now combining with my anger and grief in regard to my life, which was drastically changing. I gained weight, a lot of it. Without the ability to work out, my body wasn't able to maintain the weight I even struggled to maintain when I was able to work out. I started to really hate my life. I had survived so much but then elected to take a shot that ended everything I ever really worked for.

If I could've gone back in time, I realized I would choose to just roll back over in bed that morning and go back to sleep. This life to me just didn't seem to be worth it anymore. I struggled to just walk; what kind of life is ahead for me? Even though I made a choice to call 911 that morning, which would have indicated that somewhere deep in my mind I had a desire to survive. But now? I was regretting that decision. And things weren't yet over for me.

I was sitting on my couch one afternoon, having come home from the gym after swimming. I suddenly felt as if my foot was swelling up for some reason. It really did seem to be swelling. I wasn't sure why, but I put my foot up to try to help. Two weeks later, I would be back in the hospital.

What started in April didn't make sense to me. I was working with the physical trainer, and I kept noticing my left foot didn't want to fit in my sneaker. It didn't make sense. I didn't hurt my foot; I just would shove the foot into my shoes or sneakers and went about my business. At work, I wore duty boots twice a week as I was teaching a class with firearms and needed boots for the outside range. The boots were rather big and wide so my foot fit. My dress boots started to get tight, and I started to have a hard time zipping them up. Nothing made sense.

I started to notice my left leg seemed a little swollen as well. I wasn't in pain; it wasn't that noticeable so I didn't pay a lot of attention to it. I figured this might just be another side effect to the shot. Then came that Saturday morning. There wasn't any specific pain associated with the sudden swelling other than the top of my foot feeling tight. I elevated the foot, used ice packs, and continued about my life. Things started to get worse. I started to notice as a reddish, warm-to-the-touch pyramid seemed to be growing out of the side of my left foot. I thought it might have been a spider bite, and I tried to pop it, thinking there might be something to drain, it didn't pop.

Two weeks later after the red warm pyramid on my foot failed to subside, I called the doctor again and headed into the office. She was confused by my foot as well. Originally, she thought it might have been a gout attack. I have higher uric acid levels in my blood and always have. I take some medication for it as well. I have never had an actual gout attack, so I have no idea what that is supposed to be like. I thought that it usually caused issues for the toes and not the side of the foot, but I was willing to go with that suggestion. My doctor suggested an X-ray at the last minute. As the X-ray technician took the first picture of my foot, she immediately asked if I had hurt my foot somehow, and I told her "not to my knowledge."

She indicated that there was an obvious deformity in my foot. I looked at the X-ray, and I was completely flabbergasted at the picture. It looked like the bone attached to the pinky toe had been crushed. I didn't have anything fall on my foot. I drove home laughing most of the way; here I was walking around with a broken foot, for who knows how long, and completely unaware of it. That's when my phone rang. My doctor was calling me back. She told me she needed me to go to the emergency room. I didn't understand at first. I told her I could just come back in for a cast or a boot another day if she wanted me to. She told me that the radiologist suspected I had an infection in that foot. So I packed a bag again, a little better than I did the first time, and off to the hospital I went. This time, I drove myself.

I asked my doctor to let the hospital know I was coming so when I walked into the emergency room, they would be expecting me. The reception area was expecting me, but the doctor wasn't. When I was brought into an emergency room, the doctor eventually came in and asked what I was being seen for that day. I didn't really know the details; my doctor was supposed to send them, so I told the doctor that apparently my foot was broken. She immediately said that I didn't need to be seen in the ER for a broken foot, and I jumped right back up off the bed and said I would be happy to leave. Then someone pointed her to the note from my doctor and I heard, "Ohhhhh yeah, you do need to be here."

After multiple vials of blood were taken for cultures and being given an IV with antibiotics immediately, I finally got a chance to ask the nurse what it was that I was dealing with. She told me that I was suspected of having osteomyelitis, which was an infection but that it really tended to be an aggressive infection. I kept getting peppered with questions as to whether I had some kind of cut on my foot or some kind of wound on my foot, and my answer was no every time. Someone said that maybe I had stepped on something at some point. I don't recall stepping on anything that would have pierced my foot. But everyone seemed to just accept that I had an infection based on the X-ray that had been taken.

I was told they had paged podiatry and that I needed to go for an MRI but that the scanner was busy for the time being and I would have to wait. The podiatry resident arrived in my room and took a look at my left foot. He again asked questions about cuts or wounds to my foot recently. I told him no. He then asked if I had a cut maybe anywhere else on my body recently that was infected or didn't heal. I showed him the only injury I had at the moment. One of my cat's murder mittens connected with my arm and left a scratch, but in no way was it infected.

I was told by the resident that the on-call podiatrist was ending his on-call status that evening, and a new one was going to be on duty the next day. He said the doctor coming on duty usually acted pretty aggressively with these types of diagnoses, and he would probably do surgery. There was some discussion of what I had eaten that day as if they wanted to do surgery that night, but they decided to do the MRI first before cutting my foot open.

I sat there on the emergency room gurney; I couldn't believe what was happening. I went from just going to the doctor for what I thought was a spider bite to being in the emergency room being scheduled for emergency surgery within a couple of hours.

After hours of waiting in the ER, I was finally taken to the MRI scanner. I've never had an MRI before, and at this point, I hope to never have one again. I haven't had to do anything as painful as that in a long time. I am not claustrophobic, and there is no real reason why I couldn't lie in the tube while my foot was scanned without an issue, but there was a problem. They wanted my foot in the middle of the tube, while lying on the MRI scanning bed. My left leg was in the most awkward position because it had to be straight and pushed to the left, which put a strain on my knee and my hip and my back to the point where I couldn't take the pain anymore. I thought I was almost done, only to be told I had to do twenty more minutes this time with contrast.

I couldn't stay in the same position. I had to move. I was able to relieve the pain for a while, but then, I had to lay back down and again sit at that awkward angle and I barely lasted five minutes before I was shaking and crying from the pain. I don't want to deal with that kind of torture again. Maybe one day, someone can think to invent a bed that allows someone to lay flat and still get their foot scanned without putting so much pain into the back.

After the scan, I headed up to a room on the third floor. I was one floor below where I had been just eight months earlier. I am a fifty-one-year-old woman and the only time I spent more than one night in the hospital I was three. Now this year in just one calendar year I was back in the hospital what would be for five days ultimately and facing surgery. How do I have two hospital stays in one year?

When I got there, I asked if I could get something to eat since I hadn't had anything or any water since about 11:00 a.m., and it was now 7:30 p.m. I was finally allowed to have something to drink as they apparently decided not to do surgery that night but wait for the next day; of course, no one informed me. Alas, I was told that the kitchen was already closed. The nurse told me she had some boxed lunches, so I got a piece of turkey lunch meat, some pretzels, and a cookie. It was very good but left me still extremely hungry. I was informed I would have surgery the next day, Saturday. I was told that I needed to make sure I didn't have anything to drink or eat after approximately 6:00 a.m. So not only was I still hungry, but I wouldn't be allowed to eat the next day either.

I slept most of the night, and when I woke up on Saturday morning, it was already too late to order anything for breakfast. I drank a few glasses of water, and I just watched TV as I waited for them to come to get me for surgery.

As the minutes ticked by, it turned into hours. I couldn't go far since I was attached to an IV. I probably shouldn't be walking on the foot that was apparently broken either, so the only thing I had to do this time was to watch TV. At least on this trip to the hospital, I brought a book. I should have brought four.

At one point in the morning, the hospitalist showed up in my room. He showed me the MRI picture on the computer screen across the room. He indicated that he didn't read them much but that it appeared there was in fact some kind of abscess in my foot. I could see what appeared to be a little bubble in the picture between the fourth and the pinky toe. Sure enough, it seemed like something was, in fact, there. I even read the MRI report in my records. The radiologist had measurements for the abscess that was in my foot. The report also indicated that he saw infection in my fourth, third, and second toes.

Finally, I was told at 2:00 p.m. that I would probably be in surgery around three, which then turned into four and then five. I finally was taken to pre op where I again had to answer the same questions over and over again. This is when I first met the podiatrist who was going to do the surgery. He came in to examine my foot he was, in fact, a very nice man. But then he said, "We will try to save your toe."

Wait one minute...when did an amputation become part of the conversation here? I was just told that they would have to go in and get the infection cut out or drained out or something; no one ever said anything about losing a toe. What I didn't know at the time was not only could I have lost my toe, depending on the extent of the infection I could have lost more than one toe, I could have lost my whole foot; I could have lost part of my leg as well. It was all going to depend on how far the infection had moved. I didn't know this at the time, and I am rather perturbed that the information was rather hidden from me.

Eventually, I was wheeled into surgery, and it was lights out. When I regained consciousness, I was in post op, and a nurse had some ice chips for me. I saw my foot bundled up and a big, black surgical boot. I was told I could not take off the dressing, which was fine, as I wasn't going anywhere really quickly anyway. I was wheeled back up to my room and finally given a chance to order dinner before the kitchen closed.

One of the things that seemed to confuse all my doctors was how I didn't seem to have any pain in my foot. It didn't hurt to touch; it didn't hurt to put on a shoe. But now it hurt. After surgery, whatever they did to my foot, now it hurt, and it hurt a lot. Of course, they offered to give me oxycontin as a pain reliever, I had asked for Vicodin because Oxy gives me the spins. What I had to settle for was Tylenol, which was not enough for the pain I was in.

Getting up and down to go to the restroom was particularly painful. I eventually spotted a stool in the room with wheels. You know the kind that doctors will often use. I put that by my bed, and so any time I had to get to the bathroom I would just get out of bed, sit on the stool, and roll my way over to the bathroom. The nurses thought it was pretty entertaining.

The next day, I saw the resident again. He informed me that he had spoken to me after I was out of surgery, but he wasn't sure I would remember, and I didn't. He explained to me that they were rather confused about the surgery. He said when they opened my foot, they couldn't find an infection. My foot was definitely broken, and it appeared as if the bone had been crushed. They had to extract pieces and shards of bone out of my foot. They cleaned out my foot really well, he said, and they took a biopsy of the remaining bone to see if there was anything that would show up there.

    I didn't understand. He said they didn't really understand either. I obviously was going to need to have surgery to clean up that foot bone and the pieces of it, but I probably didn't necessarily need to have emergency surgery on a Saturday afternoon, especially if there was no sign of an infection. Now modern medicine is just fine, but I have a hard time believing just twenty-four hours of IV antibiotics cleared up an infection that seemed to be throughout my entire foot. The antibiotics generally don't work that fast, and this infection was something that everyone was very concerned about since it is hard to treat.

    I simply was at a loss. I could only think of two things that explained this situation. One that the radiologists who read my X-ray and MRI were wrong. The radiologist who read the MRI knew that the radiologist who read the X-ray diagnosed infection. So maybe the second one just confirmed a faulty diagnosis. Or maybe somehow, they had gotten the wrong films for my foot. Either way, at this point, I am extremely suspicious of radiologists.

    Two, prior to surgery, there was a very nice housekeeping staff member at the hospital who came into my room. She was actually a preacher at a local church and worked at the hospital on the side. She asked if she could pray for me before surgery. I told her that it would be very nice of her to do so, and I thanked her when she was finished. My thoughts are that somehow this woman was some kind of angel in disguise. Maybe she was sent to heal my foot. I have no other explanations, and I tend to like this explanation better. The previous one just makes me really concerned to the type of medical training radiologists are getting today.

    If she had been an angel in disguise or someone who was sent to do God's work and heal my foot, either way, something happened in that room that day. I didn't lose my foot hours later even though the infection seemed to be throughout my foot. Did God really send someone to heal me?

I spent Sunday in the hospital. On Monday, some of the test results started to come back. All the blood labs were coming back negative. No infection. The biopsy came back negative with no infection. Unfortunately for me, the test results were not enough to get me out of the hospital, at least not yet. On Tuesday, I was in no mood to remain in the hospital. The tests were coming back normal; the surgeons couldn't find infection. Why was I being kept in the hospital?

I made it clear to the resident that I was not happy to still be in the hospital late Tuesday morning. There just was no reason I was there. When I was in this same hospital with COVID and almost dead, I only stayed six days in the hospital. Here we were on the fourth day. The resident tended to agree with me. He even said when he picked up the list of patients he needed to see, his heart dropped when he saw my name still on the list. I think he decided to really push my release, and I was finally told about noon that I was going to be let go as soon as they could get me my discharge instructions.

I had to take an oral antibiotic for a week after getting released. But I was finally ready to go approximately 2:00 p.m. that day, finally. I was wheeled out of the hospital for the second time in less than a year. I was asked to walk to my car as soon as I was out of the hospital door. That was quite painful as I wasn't parked very close to that door.

I struggled with pain in the next few weeks. I tried as best as I could to keep my foot up and walk as little as possible. This of course was made easier by the fact that the semester was over, and I was off for the summer. I did struggle with my newest of my new realities. Now not only did I have an issue with figuring out where my life was going after COVID and being disabled by the vaccine, now I am actually physically disabled with a hole in the structure of my foot. I was missing part of the fifth metatarsal.

I got my bandages replaced one week after surgery. My incision was still bleeding, not in an extreme way, but everything looked normal at that point. I got my first picture of what my foot looked like through an X-ray. I actually was entertained by the picture. I had what I started to refer to as a free-floating toe, being the pinky toe. I put the picture on my cell phone and sent it to people. Most of the responses were similar to the things I was wondering: *What in the world?*

The doctor and I decided to leave the stitches in for a couple more weeks since the incision was in my foot. I have had stitches removed too soon before only to regret when the incision opened back up, so knowing it was my foot I wanted to leave the stitches in as long as I needed to. This meant, of course, I couldn't swim for the next three weeks. All the work I put in over the last eight months was going to be erased since I have to basically just sit for a few weeks.

One of the bigger challenges I had was being able to shower. I became quite the expert and tying plastic bags over my leg in order to avoid the stitches getting wet. I didn't feel safe in my home shower so I made big use of my gym membership even though I couldn't really work out much since swimming was off limits. I did use a lot of hot water in their showers for a few weeks.

I finally got the stitches out after three weeks, and I was able to do anything I really wanted at that point including swimming. I was definitely ready for trying to again get back to something I saw as normal, but what I wasn't ready for was the realization as to how important that missing bone is to the structure of the foot to the health of my knee, hip, back, neck, and making it even harder to walk as if the vaccine didn't do enough in that area already.

I immediately started to feel pain in my knee when I walked. This was different than the pain I was feeling from the vaccine; this was sharp. It was making walking so difficult. All I could focus on was the pain I was in, day in, day out. Pain from multiple sources and the pain was getting so intense. The more I tried the worse it hurt. I eventually asked to be sent to physical therapy because something had to give.

Within one appointment, the therapist was pretty sure I had a partial meniscus tear, which could have happened at any time in my past. I danced from the time I was three until I was eighteen. I ran many, many miles when I worked as a police officer and then there was a lot of running as well, training for triathlons. She was pretty sure it wasn't a complete tear so there wouldn't be a need to fix it at that point. I wouldn't have been able to stomach the idea of another surgery and another hospital stay. The most amazing thing that happened though is she taped my foot up to give me the stability of that missing bone, and suddenly, the knee pain was gone. It was instantaneous. I was never so happy, but I knew there just wasn't going to be a way to tape up my foot every day for the rest of my life.

I needed to find something that could do something to support my foot but also be something that could be put on and taken off. The therapist talked with prosthetic experts; they didn't really have an answer; if necessary, they would end up having to create something for me. I don't know if I would have the money for that. The therapist was at a loss for anything else. She recommended finding a second podiatrist for a second opinion on whether there was anything that could fix my foot. That appointment would just lead to more mystery.

I met a second podiatrist who ended up having an entirely different diagnosis for my foot. Did all the radiologists really mess up the diagnosis? Did the first podiatrist make a mistake? I didn't actually really believe this second podiatrist either. There were just things that didn't make sense. From not having pain to having pain after surgery. From how damaged the bone seemed to be to the diagnosis assuming a simple break. From my doctor thinking I had an infection but there wasn't ever anything that indicated I had an infection. I never had a cut; I never had any bruising from the break. Nothing was making sense.

It had only been a little more than a few months, and I realized I was never going to get a firm answer on my foot. I still didn't feel like I had any direction for my life after my near-death experience from COVID, and I still was not yet coming to terms with the possibility that my foot and the vaccine are going to leave me physically disabled for the rest of my life.

I did get a brace for my foot. Every morning for the rest of my life, I will now be putting on a brace as I try to cinch my foot back together and support it enough to walk. The second podiatrist did a new X-ray on my foot and discovered that the remaining bones in my foot were started to shift and move to make up for the missing bone. That was causing pain and causing more damage to the structure of my foot. Additional breaks to the foot could eventually lead to the amputation that was possible only weeks ago.

I was done. I couldn't do anymore doctor's visits. I barely survived COVID, and I hadn't yet put my life back together when the vaccine did serious physical damage to my body, preventing me from being able to put my life back to what it used to be. Now my foot was damaged, which was putting even more strain on me being able to try to walk or do anything about getting back to normal. I was so far from feeling normal I didn't know which way to turn.

One of the things I could do was read and to research. The things I have learned or at least have tried have started to make my life a little easier and help with the acceptance of all that has happened to me. I started to hear about people who had vaccine injuries. Not through any major media outlet but through places like the *Epoch Times* and through word of mouth. I was informed that a doctor here in Iowa was working with hyperbaric chambers for those who were vaccine-injured. I immediately scheduled an appointment with him via Zoom.

I explained what I had been through with COVID and the vaccine. He suggested that I might benefit from some hyperbaric chamber treatments. During spring break, I drove to his office and participated infive5 treatments. After the first, the sharp pain that existed every day all day in the back of my left leg seemed to be gone. The staff indicated that it might come back but that with more sessions, it might continue to be less at least than what it was. I had already planned four additional sessions, so I was interested to see how well things would go.

I finished five treatments in that doctor's office and five additional treatments in a hyperbaric chamber I found locally. The constant pain that was in my left leg did eventually return, but it did seem that with the oxygen therapy, it subsided at least for a brief time. The use of my legs has only improved minimally and may never get better.

I still walk slowly. I walk with a limp. When I have to walk for any distance, I now have to use a cane or a knee scooter. Stairs are extremely difficult for me to get up or down. I now know there are others who are wheelchair bound by their vaccine injury. I don't struggle that much yet. I don't know if things are going to continue to diminish in terms of usefulness.

I have used infrared light therapy all along. It helps but it isn't the entire answer. I met another doctor, Reed Pryor, who was starting to use lasers in treatment of those who suffer stroke maladies. He uses a laser device that emits green and purple laser light. I had the opportunity to use the device for a couple of weeks. It also took the pain I experience away. I will wait to see if the pain comes back, but for the first time in almost two years, I have felt more like normal. I have been walking better than I have for two years. I remain hopeful that the laser might help long term.

What is interesting about the individuals I have found who were actually willing to try things to help those of us who were vaccine injured is they are not part of the "medical community." One doctor had to leave his practice and start over to offer the hyperbaric chamber option.

The doctor with the green and purple laser is a chiropractor. During the COVID outbreak, it was chiropractors who recommended things like Ivermectin and hydroxychloroquine. Doctors who were speaking out against the CDC and the Fauci "way" of doing things were also being maligned. That should have been our first clue that they were the ones who were right.

Additional information also came to light. When my doctors thought I had osteomyelitis in my foot, my white cell count was at a sixteen, and the normal WBC is generally at ten. For me though, my white cell count has been high since the first time the test was done. Doctors thought all kinds of things, but when my white cell count is high, I rarely feel sick and there has never been an explanation that any doctor could come up with. When I was told by my doctor that the WBC was at sixteen, I didn't think much of that, but that led her to believe there was an active infection in my foot.

I assume that is why the rest of the doctors also thought there was an infection in the foot. Recent information that came to light indicates that COVID-19 can result in sepsis. It most likely wasn't and never was osteomyelitis. Sepsis would be along the same lines, and sepsis would provide an answer to the swollen leg. Is it now possible that my COVID-19 infection stayed in my body, and seven months later, set up shop in my left foot and started to eat away at my foot? Was I back in the hospital because the COVID infection was still in my body doing more damage?

Is this the reason what happened about six months after COVID happened? These are answers I don't have yet, and I don't know if I can get answers to that. I have had a tendency to tell people over the last year that I am not so sure that the foot was not somehow connected to COVID. This might explain where the infection came from. Is it possible this infection also caused the damage to the bone in my foot?

The problem I have trying to get an answer to this is the fact that doctors aren't really allowed to talk about vaccine, my doctor will allow me to refer to my situation as being a vaccine injury, but she can't outwardly admit it herself. She insists I was septic when my foot was broken, but other than COVID, where did the infection come from?

There are protocols and suggestions out there for vaccine injuries, and I am taking the supplements I have heard being suggested. I will continue to use near infrared light therapy, and when I can afford it, I will continue the hyperbaric oxygen therapy. The green and purple laser seems to be a possible solution that I might be able to continue using if my pain comes back.

I feel completely lost though. I feel like the people who are supposed to have the information are not giving out any actual information. I feel like everyone is lying about the virus and the vaccine.

6

WHERE DO I GO NOW?

How can I navigate this new situation? I am alone in this, and I don't have a lot of options to depend on, to lean on. I am so far from the idea of acceptance that the amount of stress made me really start to regret that I ever called 911 the morning I was dying from COVID, and if I had the chance to go back, I wouldn't have called. I got so low, and I saw no way out. I was an active person my whole life really. From dancing to being an officer and then the triathlons, I was never going to have any of that again. What was my life going to be? What future do I have? Do I have any future at all?

I was so deprived of oxygen the morning I was dying, had I just decided to roll over that morning and go back to bed. I would have most likely been dead within hours; I would have gone into a coma and died in my sleep from lack of oxygen. I truly regret getting up that morning and calling 911. If I knew then what I know now, I would have made a different decision.

To this day, I feel horrible for this regret. If I died, I would have left my mom to deal with my house and my belongings. I saw how hard it was for her to go through my father's things when he was dying from cancer in 2012. I hate that I almost did that to her. I hate that I almost left my two precious cats as well. They would have been taken back to my sister's house most likely where they would be scared and not understand. I still regret calling 911, and I feel horrible for the realization that I would have left my fur babies all alone. I needed to start working on coming to accept this new life of mine and find a new direction or way to feel like I can still contribute to something.

That was the issue though. I had been through so much that I wasn't even sure how to get back to any sense of feeling normal again. When COVID first hit, I didn't realize what the virus was going to do to the world and to this country. I had no idea it was going to shut everything down. I teach at a community college, and when COVID started to spread, we had just started our spring semester at school. Mostly, it was my students who questioned whether we were going to have to shut down. I hadn't heard anything from the administration about that, so I doubted it. Little did I know.

Two weeks to slow the curve. That's what they said, just two weeks because they were concerned about the ability to keep up with the potential hospitalizations that were speculated to be coming. Two weeks to slow the curve. That's all just two weeks.

The day before spring break was when our college president made the decision. We were going to shut down for spring break and the week after my coworkers and I decided we were going to have lunch together before spring break. Our boss wasn't exactly pleased since we were comingling with one another.

I, along with everyone else, assumed that we would be continuing after that in person. I didn't take things home with me that I would need for later that semester. Two weeks to slow the curve— that didn't happen. As we were shut down for that two-week period, we got further information that we were going to go completely online for the rest of the semester.

We were allowed to come into our office to collect anything we would need for the rest of the semester. It was during that period of time we discovered the college had removed all toilet paper from the restrooms on campus. One, probably to prevent us from working on campus, and then of course two, because suddenly toilet paper wasn't available anywhere in the country.

Knowing that the entire world was "shutting down" was just ominous. I would sit by the big picture window in my house and watch as the neighborhood kids would play outdoors. I would wave to neighbors as they walked by with their dogs, but the whole feeling of that time was just ominous. It was almost as if there was going to be some kind of massive cloud that moved down the street, killing everything in its path and if you were outside you were going to be swept up by that cloud of virus crap.

My work was shut down. My gym was shut down, stores were closed, when you needed groceries, you could only go into a store one way and out of a store another. I resorted to simply ordering groceries online and picking them up on the side of the store so no one had to interact with anyone else. The entire time I felt as if I was alone on the planet at times. I felt as if nothing would ever be the same. I also got very tired of worrying about when I might get the virus.

It was a lot of worry for a long time since I didn't get the virus for more than a year and a half later. After everything started, getting back to normal. During the shutdown, doctors' visits were done over the phone. Life was just completely surreal. It is no wonder after getting COVID I was so ill prepared to deal with the ramifications, like the complete dismantling of my life. I think a lot of people could agree that COVID made us less capable of dealing with stress, with disappointment, with pain, or with other people. I always saw myself as resilient. I always saw myself as being able to stand on my own two feet. The shutdown, I think, changed that.

I couldn't think of anything to do with my life after COVID. I wasn't given a new lease on life at this point, I was left with a complete blank. I felt like I didn't have anything to look forward to. COVID did that. Add to COVID the debilitating effects of the vaccine and the physically altering of my life through the foot surgery. How was I supposed to now put my life back together?

I was so angry. During the shutdown, the only exercise I could get was to ride my bike. So I did. Day in and day out, I rode my bike. It was something I could do where I could push myself to go a little harder and a little longer every day. It was something I had control over.

In a world where I couldn't control anything I had control over this one little part. I actually devised a lot of things during the shutdown I could control. I refused to pick up my phone or turn on a TV until I had ridden my bike, showered, dressed, read for at least an hour, then and only then would I allow myself to sink into the mindless time waste of watching television. I binged-watched all twenty-seven seasons of *The Amazing Race*. I watched entire series streaming things like *Ally McBeal*, *The Practice*, and other nineties TV shows that were available.

I learned to try to control as much as I could during the shutdown. After COVID, I didn't seem to be able to control anything. Nothing seemed to make sense either. Life was turned upside down with COVID and its aftermath. And it is that aftermath that I am still trying to figure out and accept. I am still angry. I am so mad at the people who created this virus. I am so angry at the people who created a vaccine that wasn't really a vaccine and how they hid the side effects. I am so angry at people who pushed that vaccine as well. I felt so much pressure from my job I am angry at those decision-makers.

I didn't like the way my job was threatened. I didn't like that it was those of us who delayed in taking that shot were treated like second class citizens. I am still more than disgusted at the pusher in charge the Dr. Fauci who apparently stood to make money off the supposed vaccine and the more he could force into it the more money he seemed to be in line for (Kennedy 2022).

One of the worst parts of the anger is that I didn't know where to place that anger. I am unable to tell the "fauci" myself just how much damage he did to my life by funding the research that created the virus and then pushing a vaccine he should have known wasn't really going to work.

Who can I be angry at? My job? I can't be angry with them, or I won't be employed very long. My friends? I can't do that because it is already a very lonely world, and I don't need to make it lonelier by losing all my friends. And just to be clear, not all my friends were pushing the vaccine. I'm angry with my doctor who didn't warn me and where I received the shot the only way to get across my anger would be to find an entirely new practice. So where does the anger go?

A lot of the anger I turned inward on myself. I punished myself for not listening to my emotions and my body when I decided to sit for that vaccine. I knew it wasn't going to turn out well, but I insisted on telling myself that everything I feared was stupid. I am so angry with myself since I didn't listen to my own voice telling me no. In fact, my body was screaming at me to not do it.

I remain extremely angry with myself for my failure to listen to my own voice. I also am angry in other ways. I am angry with myself because I can't do the things I used to anymore and angry over the fact that I will never be the same again.

And now, to add to the vaccine injury, the damage done by the virus itself that I am sure over time we will discover, and now of course, I have a structural hole in my foot that I have to treat with a brace I must wear, and I have to be very careful because now other bones could break, which might cause me to lose the entire foot.

7

THE TRIP

COVID took a lot of things away from a lot of people. My life was almost taken, my physical capabilities were stolen, and what I am finding out is my independence and my lifestyle of freedom was also put into question. Before COVID, I generally would take a trip every year to a conference I loved to attend. COVID forced that conference to be canceled for a year. A second year, the dates were changed, which didn't allow me to attend.

The next year, I had a hard time leaving my own house. I was going to be gone for a week. I was going to be away from my home for a week. That idea almost paralyzed me with fear. This was really a new feeling for me. I have always been game to go somewhere, do something. I have traveled around the world a couple of times. Suddenly, there was a fear to leave my own home. I went to the conference, and this year was no different. I went to the conference, but I still felt very uneasy about it.

One of the other things I typically do is travel abroad every other year or so. The trip that had been planned for 2020 obviously was canceled; the trip was postponed for 2021, that got cancelled as well. This was the same trip I ultimately took the vaccine for which got cancelled a few times. The cruise line during COVID was selling a couple of ships and building new ships and due to COVID they didn't have enough employees to build the boats, so the trip got canceled. Then the third year after the war in Ukraine broke out, the cruise line did a very nice thing and housed refugees. The unfortunate part for me is they picked my boat to house them. My cruise was cancelled for the third time. It wasn't cancelled in time though for me to avoid the vaccine altogether.

The fourth rescheduling of the cruise started to approach, and I started to experience that same fear and panic about leaving my house. My house had become a comfortable spot for me. A safe spot. Everything I needed was there. Everything I loved was there. Yet the trip I had planned before COVID started to spread was finally upon me. I was almost too afraid to go. I hesitated. I wanted to call it off. I wanted to stay home where it is comfortable, and it is safe.

This is not the typical person I am. Every time I took a trip, I always was aware that I would miss the pets, but this time, it was different. I actually had fear and anxiety building up in my system as the day for the flight approached. My pets could feel it as well. They tended to act a little out of sorts as well as if they could feel my fear and stress.

The day came to leave, and I almost couldn't walk out of my door. I probably cried all the way to the airport, which was about an hour away. I got to my first lay over and still felt that fear in my gut. I wanted to fly back home. Plane disruptions the next day on my flight overseas did nothing to asway my anxiety. I generally have issues with flying in one form or another, but here I was, trying to get overseas for the cruise. One entire day was wiped out by the plane delay.

To add to my anxiety about leaving my home was traveling for the first time with a knee scooter to help my mobility while overseas. This was the first really big trip with the new disabilities I've acquired from the surgery, from the vaccine and from the virus as well. When the plane delay hit, we had really only one option and that was to fly the next night on a different airline, in coach seats.

One of the things I am most ashamed of myself for is the weight I have gained since the vaccine. I used to be able to work out five days a week for a couple of hours at a time. Now that didn't keep me at a size 8, not that I ever was that size, but it did keep my weight down where I could fit into economy seats on a plane and still buckle the seat belt. Now I have spent over a year not really being able to work out at the same pace and gaining weight as I go.

But since this was the only option, we decided the only way to get to the ship was that flight. I was going to have to take the risk of the embarrassment. But the bigger thing I was afraid of is how I was going to be able to sit in a seat scrunched into a small chair for eight-plus hours.

The thought of the flight was terrifying to me. I am not good at sitting still. I am not good at sitting in one position for eight hours. I was traveling with a friend, Suzanne, and we managed to get seated in the same row. I felt a little more comfortable about the flight since it wouldn't bother her if I had to sit a little into her seat. Being able to work out was the only way I could really keep weight off. I can't work out the way I used to, and now I know what happens when I can't.

The flight was painful. I felt bruised by the time I got off the plane. I have very long legs and the seat hits me just in the wrong spot on the backs of my legs. I had bruises there. I had bruising from the armrest. I managed to sit in the window seat and sleep part of the time. I only got up once to use the restroom, and by then, we were within ninety minutes of landing. I felt as if I was going to be capable of finishing that flight. I was so relieved.

This trip wasn't starting out the best, but I was in Spain and getting luggage to head to my hotel. I managed to get there. Our seats were originally in the premium economy seats, which is not as swanky as first class, but the seats are bigger. So it isn't like I didn't plan for the weight gain I have experienced. I did plan for it, but when the plane delay happened, there weren't any premium seats left to get.

I never fly overseas without flying either first, business, or premium economy because I don't want to be the person to make someone else very uncomfortable. I also want to be as comfortable as I can. I don't know what damage the vaccine had done in my body. I do fear that I have clots that have formed and the thought of being cramped in economy not being able to move around might cause a deadly embolism. I was scared getting on the plane. I almost asked to get off.

I have to generally save a long time to afford the upgraded seat, but since I know I am not able to easily sit in economy I try to avoid it if I can. This time, it wasn't an option. This change in plans for the plane made things for me even more uncomfortable emotionally. It might seem like such a small issue, but what I have come to realize is that I just don't have the same ability to ride with the punches as I once did. I used to think of myself as a "badass" who was capable of anything. After COVID I feel a little deflated.

The next challenge I would face on this trip was all the excursions I planned. In Spain, there was supposed to be a kayak adventure that got cancelled due to the flight delay. The next day was a hop-on, hop-off bus. I took a cab to get to the starting point for the bus. Typically, I will stay on the bus for the entire route the first time around. I will then select a couple of places I might want to explore a little more and on the second rotation I would get off.

On this particular route, there was one spot that interested me as far as exploring it a little bit further. But when I saw the line of people waiting to get on the bus, I got very concerned. The ability to stand now is worse than my ability to walk. I was afraid that if I got off the bus, I would get stuck waiting in a long line in the heat which would punish my body. Instead, I got onto a second hop-on, hop-off bus and toured the city again. On this tour, there was a sky ride which I wanted to do. So the second time around, I got off and made my way to the sky lift. It was a short trip, but Barcelona was a very pretty city from the air.

Once off the sky lift, I found a cab to take me back to the hotel. I was done for the day. I was hot. I was very tired, and my body was just exhausted, and it was time to get off my feet. This is what I was concerned with when coming on this trip. How much would I be able to do? How much could my body withstand. It is hard to explain the pain I feel because it isn't pain emanating from any one place. It is hard to explain when my body is done moving. It is just a feeling that my legs just won't move anymore.

I watched a podcast featuring a Dr. Malone before this trip, and the things he said about vaccine injuries seemed to make a lot of sense. He indicated the vaccine had caused clots cutting off the use of capillaries throughout the body. So when you exercise or if your heart rate is up your body doesn't have the ability to push blood flow into the capillaries. He explained that is when people hit the "wall." When the body just can't physically do anymore. It seems to make a lot of sense with the way I feel when I try to walk or bike. Over time, I have noticed as well that it is taking a toll on my ability to swim. The next day after I push myself, the pain is just too much for me to make a go of it again. I end up sleeping longer, and just not being able to move without pain.

I have been an athlete, so I know the pain associated with exercise. This pain is so not that same kind of pain. I used to enjoy the pain I felt of a good workout before the vaccine. It is a different pain now one that I can't really describe. All I know is that it prevents me from being able to be active the next day. In the case of Barcelona, the next day was going to require that I make my way onto the cruise ship to start the next part of my trip.

I took a cab to the airport, and eventually, I boarded a bus to take me to the ship. I had to sit in the airport waiting to be taken to the transport bus. When the time came, it was very difficult to make it to the bus. I had my knee scooter for use, which I didn't take the previous day on the hop-on, hop-off bus but my physical ability to get out of the airport and get to the bus was difficult.

I was well behind the rest of the group and the exhaustion was obvious to others when I did finally arrive. I knew the trip was going to be challenging to me, and so far, it wasn't starting out very well. I managed to get onto the bus and head to the cruise terminal. Once I was checked in and allowed to board, when I got to my room, I needed to rest right away. Was I going to be able to do anything on this cruise I planned?

One thing I did discover about the cruise is that carpets are harder to use a knee scooter on than flooring. Most of the ship was carpeted. It was much easier to glide through the pool area, which was flooring. Every day I was going to be challenged by carpeting throughout the ship. My room also happened to be in the very front of the boat, a lot of the activities, and all the dining was to the rear of the boat, so there was going to be a daily trek around the ship to breakfast, to the room, to the meeting place for the excursions planned, and then off the boat.

This trip also was a go, go, go all week. Early excursions off the boat, by the time the sixth day rolled around, which was to be our first day at sea, meaning there were no excursions and nowhere to go. I was exhausted and ended up sleeping until about 3:00 p.m. I managed to get up to go to dinner and a trivia game, and then I headed back to the room to go back to bed.

That's what it seems the vaccine injury does to me. If I manage to go and keep going for most of the week it catches up to me. It isn't like I don't want to get up. I just simply can't. This is another very hard thing to try to explain or to understand. I don't get it myself. As an athlete, no matter how tired I was, I generally was out of my bed early in the morning and to the gym to run, bike, and swim. I simply just can't anymore. My body just gets too exhausted and needs the sleep.

During the weeks, I am working Monday through Friday. I often find that on Saturday, no matter what my plans are, I am sleeping well into the late morning or early afternoons.

The end of the trip wasn't any easier. I planned to stay in a hotel at the last stop of the cruise and fly home the next day. Transportation was a huge issue. I ended up having to walk quite a distance. I was on my knee scooter. My bag was perched precariously on the basket on the front of that scooter. My backpack was full and heavy and then I had to try to push my suitcase to the hotel. About halfway there, my suitcase got stuck in a hole. It went over, and I went over with it, flipping over the handlebars of the scooter, landing on the suitcase, and then being pulled over by my backpack. I ended up hitting my head on the staircase I fell by.

The trip was a test; it was a test to see if I could do it. I knew it would be a challenge, and I wasn't sure I would be successful. There were a couple of times during the trip I almost investigated how to switch my flight and go home early. I often felt a bit overwhelmed at trying to do certain things. I often felt broken. I often felt like I was kidding myself for even trying this in my current state. The saddest part was the idea that if I couldn't successfully maneuver this trip. Was this the end of my ability to go anywhere?

I've been around the world a couple of times and have seen some beautiful things. Was this going to be it? I'm glad that my travels in the world started in 2013. So many people wait to travel for "someday." I am glad I didn't wait for some day because I might never have been able to see or do the things I have. If I had waited, how much would I not have been able to do?

*****

Throughout this book, I've talked about what happened to me and as you can see, I have had a lot of time to sit and think about my situation. How it happened, what it means, and where I go from here. After COVID, it took a few weeks before I felt strong enough to try to start rebuilding my workout capacity. I started with swimming, which was my favorite anyway. After a few weeks of not swimming and fighting off COVID, barely, I was dismayed when I could only do two laps without having to stop in the pool. Before COVID, I could swim a mile nonstop, thirty-five laps at least. After COVID, I barely managed two. That first day I swam two laps, rested, and swam an additional two for a total of ten, but I was completely destroyed I was barely able to move.

It took about a month, but I did manage to build my swimming back up. By the middle of November, I felt as if I was successfully able to swim a mile again. It was hard, the distance did not come easily. I started trying to build my biking back up.

I started to bike at least twice a week. I started with just ten minutes, and by the middle of December, I was up to about forty-five minutes on the bike, which usually amounts to about twelve miles. I started to work on just walking. I thought I had the swimming and the biking back. I was just starting to cross train between the bike and the swim when I added in walking.

I managed to walk almost a mile when the day came, and I took the second vaccine shot. I suddenly could no longer walk. I could only manage about five minutes on a bike, swimming was still a strength for me, but that is mostly an upper body workout. My arms didn't really seem as impacted from the shot as my legs were. The problem I had swimming would come from the exercise intolerance and the problem I had just getting out of my bed in the morning.

You can see I had a lot of time to think about my situation. Then when the infection and the surgery on my foot took place that was another few weeks I couldn't swim or do anything because I had stitches and a foot that was now broken in a different spot. I had a lot of time to consider what happened to me.

I am sure I am no different from people who have an accident and become disabled in the middle of their life. I am sure I am experiencing some of the same emotions. I am not completely disabled, but I am still, I think, experiencing some of the same emotions. Anger at so many things, hurt in terms of pain but also in terms of how this could have happened, embarrassed in how my body changed, and how I am no longer able to do sometimes some very simple things, jealous of others who never got COVID and those who got the vaccines and didn't have a problem with them. There are so many emotions tied up in me.

I am not special, and there are a number of people who I am sure are going through the exact same thing as I am. I've learned that there are about 7 percent of people who have had a reaction like I have to this vaccine. There are 7 percent of us out there, some in much worse condition than I and some in not as bad of a condition. I am not special in that way, but this is my story. I have used some of my time to reflect on my life and my future and even on my purpose.

I kept seeing certain words that drew my attention whenever I was on social media sites like Facebook. The words that just seemed to keep popping up were words like *grace*. Grace, as I did some research, could be defined as when God protects you from the bad things you don't deserve to happen to you. Did God protect me from the worst outcomes? Am I favored enough by God to deserve grace?

Words like mercy, when God protects you from bad things that you very well could deserve to have happen to you. And words like *blessings* when God is generous with both grace and mercy. I often wondered about my situation. Did I deserve this? Did I deserve to contract a virus that almost ended my life? Did I deserve this phantom infection that almost took my life a second time? Was someone trying to get my attention?

That was a comment a friend of mine made. A friend who actually once considered going into the priesthood. He specifically asked if I thought that maybe God was trying to get my attention. I've always believed in God. I grew up Catholic, but I don't generally subscribe to that religion anymore. But is faith in God something I think about daily? No. Should I? Maybe. This whole experience, though, is allowing me to revisit my faith.

After all this happened, I was in a deep despair. I can look back now and know I was going through the stages of grief. I was going through a deep depression. I was overwhelmed. I didn't know how to survive this, and I regretted calling 911 that morning. If I had just rolled over and gone back to sleep, I wouldn't have to live this way anymore.

I don't believe my situation was intentional, I don't think God sought me out to give me this virus, which impacted half of the world. The virus wasn't intentional to me, but it was still very difficult to deal with.

I have learned over time to not tempt fate. I have refused to say things like "How much more do I have to take?" Or say things like "Why me?" I learned earlier in my life when you tempt God or the universe, it's a challenge. Just when you asked how much more you have to take? God or the universe will be there to show you just how much you can handle because there is plenty to dish out.

I've worked with a couple of coaches in my life as well: Orna and Matthew. It was their help that allowed me to escape the hole I had crawled into after COVID. Honestly, the idea of not calling 911 that fateful morning and just going back to bed seemed like such an attractive alternative to the hell I was living now. I felt immense regret in having bothered to save my life. I could have just drifted off in my sleep, and I wouldn't have to live with this pain today. I wouldn't have had to keep pushing forward. I could have been done with this world.

My coaches helped me to put a ladder in that hole and climb out and to start life again. They reminded me that one of my challenges in life would be to deal with feeling overwhelmed. Boy, did I ever feel as if I was overwhelmed during the entire year long episode. I just needed to recognize when I was experiencing the feelings of being overwhelmed and then using some of my tools to counteract that feeling.

I've been very overwhelmed throughout this entire episode. I live alone, I live far away from family. I have some friends, but I try not to depend on them too much because I tend to feel as if they will stop being my friend if I ask too much of them. I have felt so overwhelmed for a long time. I have been quick to tears when faced with difficulties. I try not to, but it seems to just reach a bubbling over point quickly, so I am still working on that to this day.

8

Finally, the Fauci

The story of COVID keeps changing. I don't know what is worse the idea of dying from COVID or the idea of surviving it and finding out that my own tax dollars most likely went to help pay for the funding of the research to create the virus that infected the world in the first place.

Then I find out the exact medication I asked my doctor for before I ever got sick would probably have lessened the impact of the virus on me because it was an effective low-cost alternative. I was sold the line "hydroxychloroquine" would do more harm than good. In the book *The Real Anthony Fauci* by Robert F. Kennedy Jr., I learned the study done on that particular drug was done giving elderly patients massive doses of the drug, which did kill them. They were apparently given 2,000 mg when the actual dosage should be less than 200 mg (Kennedy 2021).

Instead of being able to take hydroxychloroquine prophylactic way, I just had to sit and wait to see if I got sick. Of course, when I did, I was treated with the CDC's more expensive treatments, which actually didn't do anything at all to fight the virus. It seemed to be a way for doctors to pad their pockets by forcing the Remdisivir, which killed many with kidney or liver failure. The Fauci tested Remdisivir starting way back in 2017 and found little to no benefit to the drug. A Chinese study of the drug found that it didn't decrease the amount of viral load in a patient's blood, nor did it reduce the length of hos-

\s. But because there was a huge financial gain coming, \bout his own study and told the world the drug showed ___ ,..ennedy 2021).

Then, of course, there was the whole Ivermectin mess. Ivermectin is a drug that was a Nobel Prize–winning drug that has a high capacity to treat parasitic infections with low to no side effects. An Australian study found that Ivermectin destroyed the viral load in a patient within forty-eight hours. The drug is available over the counter in many countries, particularly the ones that are prone to malaria (Kennedy 2021).

Doctors like mine weren't able to prescribe it. It hadn't been labeled specifically as a treatment for COVID, so it was considered off brand and there are state licensing boards who threatened to pull their medical license if they had prescribed it. Ivermectin was approved for human use in 1996. The Nobel Prize was given to the developers of Ivermectin a full five years before the COVID breakout (Kennedy 2021).

I remember the media falling in line with the idea that it was a horse dewormer. It is, it works on parasites, but the media talking heads didn't do their research or they would have found the drug has been available for human use for over two decades. The Ivermectin drug was successful in treating many people who managed to get the drug from their own doctors. One of the most famous people treated by that drug was Joe Rogan (Kennedy 2021).

The congressional hearings I watched made me sick to my stomach. To watch this person who had been trusted for decades basically unsupervised deny his part in creating the virus and then refusing to answer whether or not he financially benefitted from the treatments he recommended was just disgusting. There is no other word for it. How can someone play god like this and then take no responsibility for his actions? There is more and more evidence coming out in the way of emails and a book by Senator Dr. Rand Paul, which covers just how much the American people have had the wool pulled over their eyes. I want to wretch every time I hear him claim he had nothing to do with making me sick.

I've watched and read about the HIV and AIDS pandemic when Fauci first became a public figure. Is it any surprise the first thing he wanted to do was develop a vaccine for HIV? I find that suspicious of him. People have talked about how his treatments may have killed more people than helped. How he delayed the appropriate development of treatments. That isn't the focus of this particular book, but it would seem that there is a history of doing exactly what he did for COVID before (Kennedy 2021).

There was something called monoclonal antibodies as well that especially when combined with Ivermectin they were very successful in treating the illness. Many people talked about feeling better within two days. I was never told about either of these options by my doctor. When I got sick, I didn't know there were options that could have lessened my misery. I may have received the monoclonal antibodies in the hospital, but the doctors were very quick to put me on Remdisivir first. From what I heard that IV fluid costs only $10 to make, but insurance companies were charged $3k for each treatment, and I know I received at least five of those.

Maybe it would have been better to die than to learn all the ways I was betrayed by the very people who take an oath to "Do no harm," people put in place at the heads of agencies, being paid millions by pharmaceutical companies, to push the treatment, and then of course, the biggest betrayal of them all to find out my tax dollars funded the creation of the virus, the eventual release of the virus and then eventual contraction of the virus.

Everything in the investigation to COVID has now pointed to the idea that the Fauci, as I call him, used millions of the dollars he is designated every year by Congress to further medical research and sent millions to a company apparently called Eco Health. That company in return then funded what we now call "Gain of Function" Research in a lab in Wuhan, China. From all accounts out of Congress as of this writing, researchers in Wuhan took a bat virus from a bat only found in China and only found in a deep, dark recess of a cave in that remote part of China, and then they inserted a gene into that virus that made it more capable of attaching in humans and making it more deadly in humans. Everyone who reads this book funded that research.

I am sick to my stomach every time I think about the fact that scientists even remotely thought that this would be good science. That scientists would ever dare to play in the "God" game like this. That scientists would ever dare to make something so dangerous, so evil, so diabolical is just beyond my comprehension. I was a police officer, but I never wanted to take a life. That is something for the sociopaths in the world. Where were the ethics folks when the research was being vetted? Have all the scientific community lost their way? Have they forgotten that humans are not invincible? How did science take such a wrong turn?

These are questions I cannot answer. I know when I was attempting to write my dissertation, the daunting requirements of the IRB or Institutional Review Board when one wanted to use human subjects in research were so strict. How did this gain of function research ever get approved? Was it because researchers could use unwitting people in Brazil or Africa for their human subjects? It is completely unforgiving and unacceptable. This research could have been a planet killer. And it still could. For those who got the virus we really have no idea the kind of damage it has done to our internal organs. I suspect you will see virus victims continuing to die off at an early age.

What about those who got the vaccine? We also have no idea what those chemicals and MNRA technology is doing to our bodily systems. As I write this book, I suspect I have clots and sometimes I can feel pain in my lower leg that would seem to be related to that possible idea. The daily pain I deal with and the fact that my legs don't work anymore just tells me that there are serious problems that are sitting dormant in our bodies like a time bomb.

If my doctor months before I got sick had only given me hydroxychloroquine when I asked, maybe I wouldn't have been on death's door. If she had only given me that drug maybe I wouldn't have had to struggle to breathe for weeks. If she had only given me the drug and if I got the virus anyway maybe I could have developed immunity and not taken the shot at all. I'd still be able to walk and bike and not deal with the debilitating exhaustion and pain. If she had only given me that drug, maybe I wouldn't be here writing this book at all.

I am angry with my doctor, but sadly, like the vast majority of medical practitioners out there, she is just a member of the system. The system that determines what health people are going to receive and what information is going to be the "go to" talking point. She works for a major health system and breaking the rules could impact her family and her life. I'm still very angry. I was forced and just left to get the virus and possibly die from it before she was going to go against the rules and give me the drug that might have lessened the impact, all before I got sick.

The information I have learned after getting sick astounds me. How wrong science seems to be today. It used to be that science was supposed to improve the human condition and the world around us. Maybe science now thinks it is appropriate to determine whose lives are worth improving, and it doesn't seem to be the elderly or those with other preexisting conditions. Maybe that is the desire of science. To eliminate those of us who are less than a perfect specimen of a human being. Eliminate the ill, the elderly, and then reduce the population by not allowing them to reproduce either. The numbers of miscarriages is way up in those who were given the vaccine.

This world has changed. Science has changed. My life has changed and is still changing. I am still very angry and so many people. I have to work at forgiving my doctor for example or forgiving those who pushed me into getting the vaccine to begin with, forgiving the person who gave me the virus even though I don't know who they are. Most of all, I have to work on forgiving myself. I am so angry with myself. I didn't listen to that voice in my head that told me to stay away, to not do it. I so often tell people to listen to their instincts. Listen to the voice inside of your head that is telling you not to go somewhere with someone. Listen to the voice inside of your head, telling you that you are not in a good situation and to get out of the place you are in. That voice could very well be the voice of God cutting you off at the pass before you head down that wrong road.

But I ignored my own advice. I ignored my own inner voice that was screaming at me to not get the shot. The tears that welled up in my eyes and rolled down my cheeks every time I thought about getting the vaccine should have told me all I really needed to know. The desire to run away when the nurse came in with the vial to do the actual injection. Oh God, why didn't I listen?

I'm hurt. I am so hurt knowing I paid to help create this vaccine. I am so hurt to know that people who are supposed to be trusted like medical professionals sold us all out. I am so hurt that someone thought this would be a good idea to inflict on the world. I always tried to give human beings in a civilized world the benefit of the doubt, but I can't anymore. People have proven to be untrustworthy.

I have an entirely different life now. I can't do the things I'd like to do because of a vaccine. I can travel, but it isn't easy. I can work but it is very difficult. Someday, I might not be able to work anymore. What then? Where do I go? Who do I have to depend on? My mother is getting on in years. I have no husband to help who would stay by my side through thick or thin. I am alone on this planet, and I feel like I am in danger.

My life is never going to be the same, and I miss my old life. I miss the training for triathlons. I miss the ability to just get up and move. I miss the ability to travel where I want and do what I want to do there.

So what is the lesson in all this? The world has changed. And while you still might be able to find people who will do right by you, they seem to be fewer and fewer in between. The lockdowns or the supposed two weeks to flatten the curve as "the Fauci" liked to call it was akin to a madman playing with dolls and extracting their evil desires on those pawns. The lock down changed people as well. We don't communicate like we used to. We don't trust one another like we used to be able to. The world has fallen apart, and all it took was a virus. How fragile is the entire human race?

9

How Did I Find the Ability to Move On

I was asked one day since I was facing the things I am facing, how do I move forward? I wasn't prepared for that question. But I realized in that moment, if I was given another day to wake up then I needed somehow keep going. I know I said many times, if I had the chance to go back to that morning knowing what I know now I might have just rolled over and gone back to sleep in hopes of just slowly drifting away. But I did make the choice to call 911, so somewhere deep inside, there was some kind of desire to live.

Knowing everything going on in the world today, yes, it is scary and yes, it is disturbing; and I am afraid of the future. I don't know where this country is going, and I don't know how I am going to fare. If there is some kind of national emergency, I am as prepared as I can be, I guess.

But how do I move on? How have I been able to move forward emotionally or physically? I will admit, there have been times that I've felt completely defeated and felt as if it was over and that I just couldn't do it anymore, but slowly, I have tried not to give up. The letters I wrote to my friends and mentors kept me afloat for a while. While it fed my soul, it wasn't the whole answer. Once all the letters had been sent, I still was left sitting here in my house staring at four walls, knowing how painful it is just to try to get off the couch.

Gone is the opportunity to train for another race; I just can't. The pain is too much. Gone is the opportunity to travel and do things like walk up Mt. Vesuvius or climb to the top of the Leaning Tower of Pisa. Even the idea of being able to take a walk is terrifying. If I go for a walk, will my legs work long enough to get back? How long will it take to even get ready requiring a brace on my foot, and how much pain will I experience?

So what is it that helps me to keep going? I've always strongly believed that I had a purpose on this planet. As I look back on my life, I can see the things I have accomplished to acts I have completed that helped some and protected others. Every place I lived, I met people because I was supposed to. Sometimes the people I met were there to teach me a lesson or push my life forward. Sometimes the people I met, I was there in their life to help them move forward.

I have to believe that this history will continue, just in a new and different way. I believe that God has used my life to be in places where I was needed at the right time. I have no doubt that the future will be more of the same. Disabilities and all. Maybe my presence or these words written here will reach another person and continue my work of impacting others so that they can move forward in their life.

There are so many people out there who I have heard about who were able to take the horrible things that happened to them and turn it around. I don't know if that is my path, but maybe these words will reach people who are going through similar things and give them the knowledge that they aren't alone, which is something that I know all too well.

Maybe I am still here and still getting additional time on this earth so I can be here to see the revelations come out, giving people like me the ability to see our conditions admitted to or at least accepted. One day, perhaps, there will even be an answer to help cure those of us injured by the vaccine. So many people when I mention the words *vaccine injury* have a hard time hiding their facial reaction of disbelief as they look at me as if I am a conspiracy quack. It would be nice to see the medical community admit that what I feel and what I am going through is not in my head.

As people do, I did a deep dive into research to try to figure out why we are here on earth when I was in my twenties. I was old enough to have experienced a little bit of life, but young enough yet to know that I didn't have all the answers yet. This new life experience brings me back to the discoveries and the realizations I made almost twenty-five years ago.

Growing up Catholic, I totally agreed with being a Christian, but I wasn't quite sold on the whole fire-and-brimstone ideology, or the fact that somehow, I needed a priest to confess and be sorry for my sins. I just didn't understand why I could do that on my own.

I eventually found answers that spoke to my soul and my heart. I found solace, strengthening and actually a confirmation of my beliefs through books written by individuals like Sylvia Browne and John Edward. Now before you dismiss these individuals as fake psychics preying on people, I have read their books and what I found were deep Christian believers, John Edward even being Catholic as well.

I found individuals who wrote about things I couldn't know, but when I read their words, they just rang true to me. You can check out any of their books, and if they don't speak to you, then your answer is somewhere else. These books spoke to me.

Not only did I read their books, I also attended a couple of events they held, and while some people might dismiss their psychic capabilities, I was astounded at the amazing accuracy of all the information. Before dismissing what they did as having plants in the audience or someone in line with the rest of us asking for information, I saw no indication of that.

I've seen some physical manifestations during these events that cannot be explained and no matter how much individuals try to claim it is fake the information was, plain and simple, it was just too accurate and too specific. The events I attended gave me a lot of calm. Life does go on after this physical manifestation.

One of the things that John Edward talks about during his live sessions was the idea we were sitting in a specific place in the room for a specific reason. By the end of that session, I knew what he was talking about. I had nothing in common with the people or the families on either side of the room, but just about everything he talked about when he was working with the center section of the crowd also pertained to my family, even though he wasn't directly reading me.

It is just not possible to randomly sit in a place that corresponded to other families that experienced the same things. He also addressed those who would try to tear him down. He worded it so simply. If we can speak to relatives or loved ones who have passed on, through prayer or just talking, why can't they speak back to us? So many people believe in signs like finding dimes or pennies or seeing birds in their windows. I don't have any of these "signs" that I look for, but having lost a couple of very close friends knowing the information from my research, and these events allowed me to come to terms with where they are and knowing I do get to see them again when the time comes.

In my own illness, this was the information that allowed me to come to terms so simply with being at the end of life. I knew what was going to come next thanks to the books and the events, and some television shows and movies like *After Death*, which most recently came out in theaters in 2023.

I am not going to disclose the personal nature of the messages I heard through the events I attended, particularly with John Edward. I believe I truly received the messages through these events because they are deeply personal, but the fact remains my belief in a life after, my belief in God and Christianity was always strengthened through that experience.

The research I did alluded to the idea that we all plan out our lives on this planet, when we are born, the parents we have, the experiences we are going to face. The body we have, yes, especially my red hair. And most importantly, when we are going to return to our true lives on the other side. This also answers for me the question as to why bad things happen. If bad things didn't happen, we would never know what good can be. If bad things didn't happen, we wouldn't experience the things we planned to when we created this life.

A lot of people question, for example, why kids get sick or are killed by murderers. I am comfortable with the idea that those souls who leave the planet early don't need to be here for long. I believe those souls who leave early are also there to help their parents learn about loss and grief and how to survive that which is what they planned for their own life. Why are there seemingly bad people who do bad things? They, too, are here on this planet at this time to bring about some endings, to bring about experiences for others who had planned to learn about victimization in their plan.

I was specifically born at three forty-three in the morning on October 5, 1970, in Buffalo, New York, because that date time and place set in motion all of the things that would play out in my life, including almost dying from COVID in September 2021. I, of course, didn't know exactly what would "cause" my death, but prior to coming to earth, I planned to have what Sylvia Browne calls an exit point that day. Just like the bicycle crash I had, a few months before COVID was also an exit point which I decided not to take.

According to her books, we each plan out five different exit points in this lifetime, and we choose when we take those exits. I am darn sure when I spent days in a hospital, at the age of three in an oxygen tent due to croup and breathing problems, it was my first exit point. I cannot recall that in my conscious memory, but that experience impacted the rest of my life. I have a deep fear of doctors and such from that experience. It was meant to happen and it as for me to understand the trauma and deal with that trauma. Although, I am successful only occasionally controlling my panic. But could this have been a reason I delayed calling a doctor when I got sick during COVID? Was it a reason I delayed calling 911 when I was suffocating to death?

The second and third exit points came in the year of COVID. The bike wreck was very strange. I had just taken off my helmet while riding because a bug got stuck in one of the air vents. I was very close to home, and as I put the helmet back on, I didn't snap it together. Something bugged me about that; divine intervention? Maybe. I worked to snap the helmet shut while still riding so I needed to do it with one hand, which made it difficult. I managed to get it snapped just as I saw the dog. The little, tiny dog running at my bike. The dog attacked my front wheel, going under the wheel and under the chain, throwing me over my handlebars and onto the ground. If

I hadn't snapped the helmet when I did, I never would have survived the crash as I landed pretty much on my head.

I had a concussion. I knew that I broke a tooth in my mouth I hit so hard. Without that helmet, I wouldn't have ever gotten COVID. I probably would have died right there on the bike path. Was it just coincidence that I snapped the helmet? Was someone pushing me from a place I can't see or hear to do it? Did someone intervene knowing that this was an exit point for me? Was it God himself warning me? When you believe in the unseen and unheard, there very well could have been some divine intervention involved in pushing me to get the helmet strapped together and firmly on my head because I felt deep down inside what was about to happen, even if I couldn't consciously know.

COVID then, of course, becomes the third point of exit for me. I don't know that I have two more exit points at this time. The car crash could have been so much worse and could have also been a point of exit. I might be down to my last exit, meaning, I am also down to my last opportunities to impact the world around me.

Even though I might be at my last exit, although I still speculate I have two, it isn't a scary thought. It is that thing that gives me drive again honestly. I might have a shorter time than most to impact the world, but I still can, and I have an opportunity to do so. I also just planned a trip to go to Antarctica.

Reading the books I did, things just always seemed to "make sense" to me as if I knew this was the right information. I somehow knew deep in my heart and soul this information was somehow the truth. The books often corroborated each other. Some of the artists renderings in Browne's books hit deep down. I always felt as if I had seen these things before, I had been in these places before.

Their books and even other books by other authors I've read all generally confirmed for me the things my soul always seemed to know. There is a God. Jesus was his son who died on the cross for our sins. This earthly life is the illusion. This life is for us to "learn" and then return to our real home with the lessons we have learned to share with God since he is not man and cannot experience things like grief, happiness, depression, or joy as a human does.

Based on my research, my life on earth is focused on experiencing an array of emotion. Experiencing a number of careers. I've worked in radio, I was a law enforcement officer, and I am now a college professor. I was a dancer, I was an athlete, and now I am something I have yet to define.

Experiencing a number of situations that not surprisingly were rather common to each other. We all seem to have specific patterns and once we learn to handle the challenges put in front of us, it can become easier. But the challenges you face will always tend to be in the same category. I had to move around the country, and I often had to say goodbye to people I loved. I often had to learn to make new friends, I always had that challenge to try to continue the friendships that are distance relationships only to find time and time again they just don't seem to work.

I often have to deal with feeling overwhelmed. Whether I was trying to move with a U-haul and a trailer with my car on it. Whether I was trying to learn how to navigate a new city, all before GPS. Whether I was learning a new job or new role. I've felt overwhelmed financially at times, emotionally at times, and now I feel overwhelmed physically, but that isn't going to stop me.

I've learned a lot moving and having to say goodbye to people I loved, it is one of my life challenges. I've lost dear friends this way. The preparation with losing those friends prepared me for the overwhelm I would feel when one of my best friends, confidants, and coworker would die completing a suicide, which was particularly hard to take I knew he would end his life, he told me so. It was still heartbreaking, overwhelming, and disturbing the day he left this planet because I still hoped he would stay. Time and time again though, I've had this life theme of saying goodbye. To be honest it doesn't really get any easier, but I've survived it so often that I know friendships might not last forever. That is why we need to get the most out of our friendships while we still have them.

If Sylvia Browne were to label it, she would tell you I am an "experiencer" here on earth to take part in a lot of different careers, in a lot of difference places, learning each time how to live, love, and then eventually to move again and have to learn to say goodbye each time.

COVID may have opened up a new path for me. While I am still an "Experiencer," I am now writing about my experience to help others, those who have maybe lost their own way after COVID. Others who may have been injured by vaccine to help them to find a new way to live and to find the ability to handle the pain and the disability, to handle the emptiness in their soul and to find a way to fill their life with joy again.

This is my new path. I don't have to climb Mt. Everest. I don't have to move again or switch careers again. I am able to now share my story. I am able to help others who have found themselves in the same place I was and honestly still am. I definitely don't have all the answers, but I understand it now. I understand that this is just another experience along my path. Just like I am able to impact my student's lives most of the time, if not all the time, for the better; now I have the chance to reach people on a wider scale.

Experiencing is precisely what my life has been. I experienced growing in a family with siblings, and often, we struggled for money. I experienced having to start working at a young age, to always have a job and to always be self-sufficient. In my lifetime, I have only had to file for unemployment once, and I accepted a check literally for two days because by day three I had new job to tide me over until I could find a better full-time position to take.

I experienced having to say goodbye to so many friends and lives as I hurdled through this life seemingly on a timeline, which I apparently planned before I arrived here on earth. I haven't struggled paycheck to paycheck at times. At other times, I have stressed about every dime in my bank account. We all have paths to live in this life. We have things to do and things to experience.

I always was in a certain place at a certain time to interact with certain people and experience very specific things and sometimes that required that I move halfway across the country. I lived in Buffalo, New York, growing up, went to college in Pennsylvania, worked for a company during my summer months which took me to New Hampshire and to Ohio, worked in Michigan, Missouri,

Wyoming, and then to Iowa. Each time, I met people I was supposed to meet, did things I was supposed to do, learned things I needed to learn and then I moved on.

When I actually started trying to follow the advice of the research I did decades ago, I focused on meditations I tried my best to listen to any of the signs that might be around. I actually at one point predicted that my life was again about to change drastically, although I didn't know how yet, but it was within the next few days that I would lose a job and have to move again and start all over in a new place. I needed to go because my life was moving forward. The lives of my friends I was leaving also needed to move forward without me. They have their path, and I have mine.

As it happens, when you get busy sometimes you just believe you don't have the "time" to follow through on the things you should. I lost a little bit of my connection with all the research I had done. Perhaps COVID was the impedes that was designed to put me back on track. Although it has been a long road, I firmly now believe that yes COVID might be God trying to get my attention again.

It is time to get back to my study my meditation and self-reflection. We all have a specific start in this life. Our lives are what we choose to do with them. We still have free will as to whether we follow our path or not, we don't plan out every second before we get here. We plan the major events; we plan the patterns that show up in life. What I know is that we all also have a specific end. We don't know when that time comes. I believed that COVID would be my end, but here I am still. I don't know what's to come in my future. All I can do is to try to keep going and knowing every day is a chance to have an impact on the world.

References

Browne, Sylvia. 1999. *The Other Side and Back*. Carlsbad, California: Hay House Publishing.
Edward, John. 2003. *After Life, Answers from the Other Side*. Carlsbad, California: Hay House Publishing.
Kennedy, Robert F. Jr. 2021. *The Real Anthony Fauci*. Delaware: Skyhorse Publishing.
Paul, Rand. 2023. *Deception The Great Covid Cover-Up*. Washington, DC: Regnery Publishing.

Picture Section

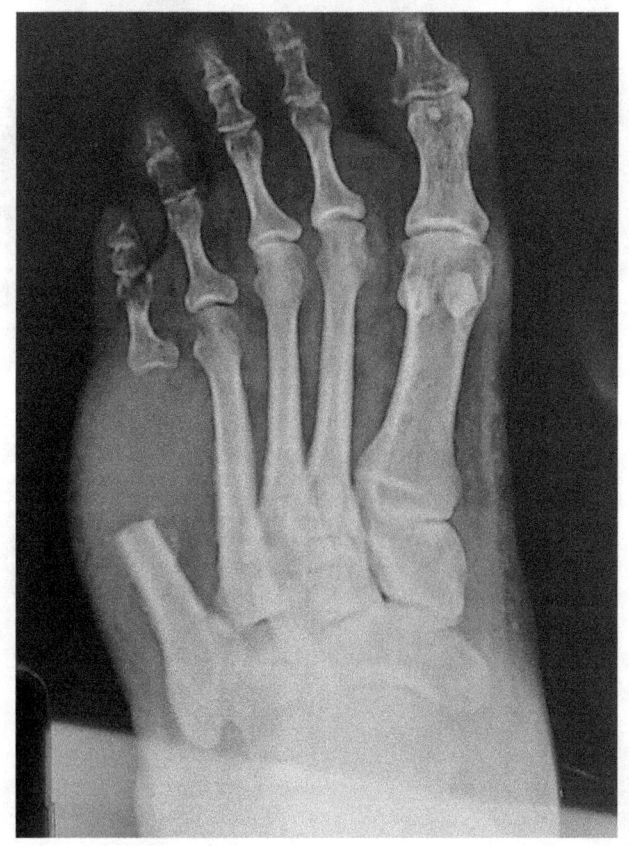

THROUGH THE COVID LOOKING GLASS AND BACK

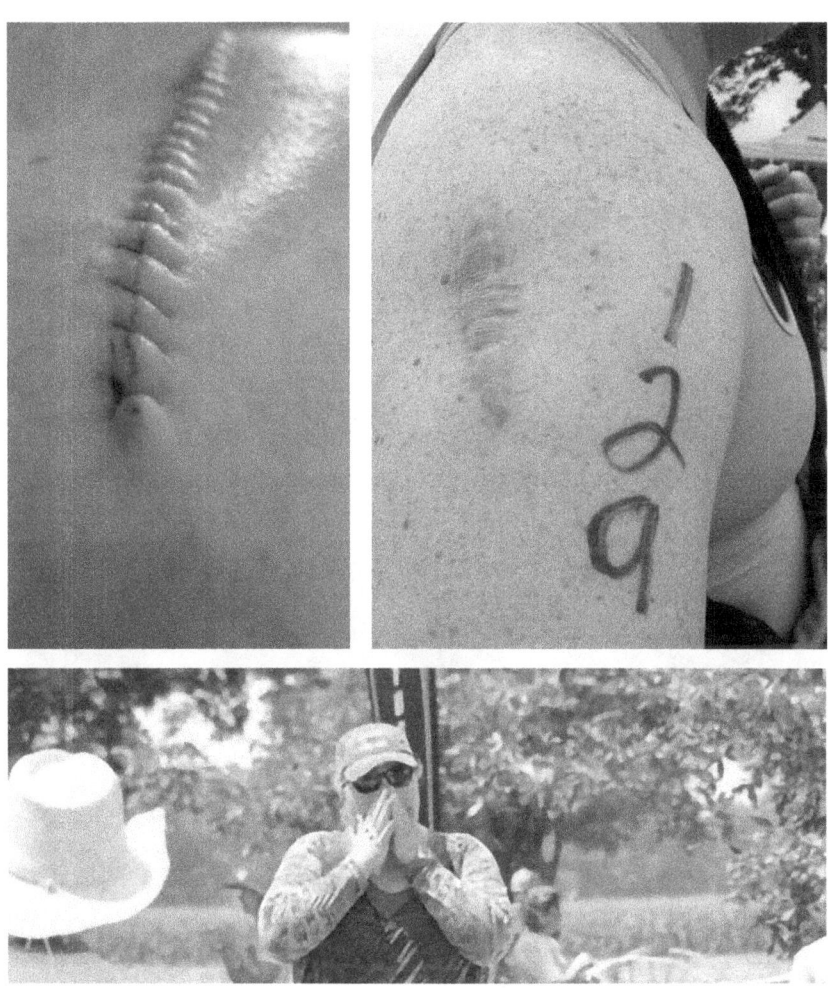

THROUGH THE COVID LOOKING GLASS AND BACK

About the Author

A native of the Buffalo, New York area, Traci grew up in a family of four kids. Early on, she had an interest in radio and television. After college, she started her career at WBEN radio. After working in Buffalo, New York, moving onto Iron Mountain, Michigan, and then eventually Jefferson City, Missouri, she discovered she had a true calling to do something different. She attended a police academy and started working as a police officer in Missouri in August 1999. After finishing a master's degree in criminal justice and continuing her postgraduate education, she found herself leaving full-time law enforcement and moving into education both online and in a community college setting. There she taught students about law enforcement and the criminal justice field. She has graduates in a number of different fields one is an attorney, another is attending law school, one in the coast guard, a couple in the navy. Many of her former students are currently practicing officers. She spent twelve years in Wyoming and then relocated to Iowa and continues in the same education role today. It was in Iowa where this particular story begins and continues to take place.

Printed in the USA
CPSIA information can be obtained
at www.ICGtesting.com
JSHW022107250524
63589JS00004B/15